# English Unlimited

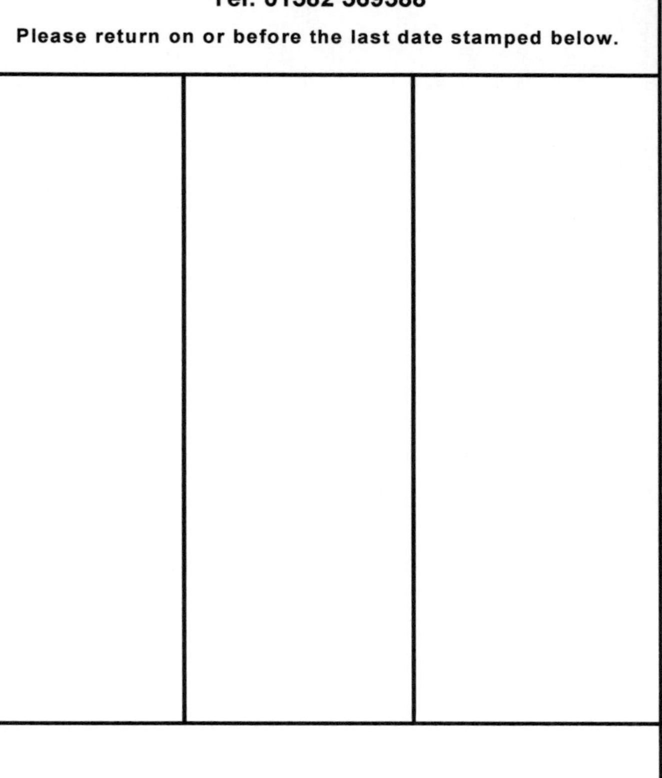


## A1 Sta
Sel -ROM)

Adrian Doff

CAMBRIDGE
UNIVERSITY PRESS

University Printing House, Cambridge CB2 8BS, United Kingdom

One Liberty Plaza, 20th Floor, New York, NY 10006, USA

477 Williamstown Road, Port Melbourne, VIC 3207, Australia

314–321, 3rd Floor, Plot 3, Splendor Forum, Jasola District Centre, New Delhi – 110025, India

79 Anson Road, #06–04/06, Singapore 079906

Cambridge University Press is part of the University of Cambridge.

It furthers the University's mission by disseminating knowledge in the pursuit of education, learning and research at the highest international levels of excellence.

www.cambridge.org
Information on this title: www.cambridge.org/9780521726344



First published 2010

20 19 18 17 16 15 14 13 12 11

Printed in Dubai by Oriental Press

*A catalogue record for this publication is available from the British Library*

ISBN 978-0-521-72634-4 Starter Self-study Pack (Workbook with DVD-ROM)
ISBN 978-0-521-72633-7 Starter Coursebook with e-Portfolio
ISBN 978-0-521-72638-2 Starter Teacher's Pack
ISBN 978-0-521-72636-8 Starter Class Audio CDs



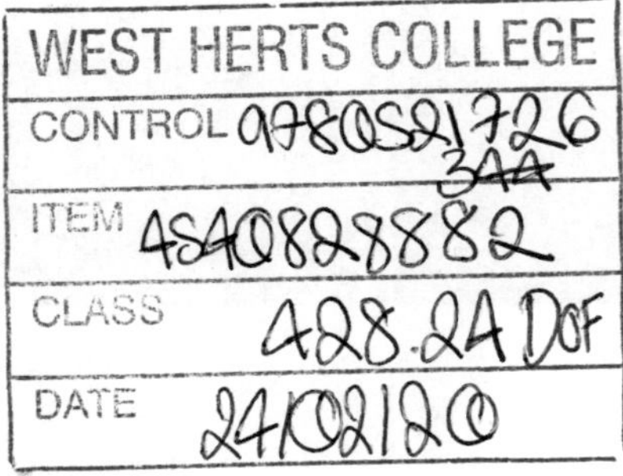

# Contents

# 1 Hello

**VOCABULARY**
*Hello, I'm, My ...*

**1** **Write the words in the gaps.**

~~my~~ from I'm name meet from I'm to I'm

**BILL** Hi. 1 *My* 2 ______ is Bill Green. 3 ______ 4 ______ New York.
**LARS** Hello. 5 ______ Lars Svenson. 6 ______ 7 ______ Oslo.
**BILL** Oh, yes. Nice 8 ______ 9 ______ you.

your I'm Nice My you

**KATIE** Hi, I'm Katie. 10 ______ a student here.
**BOB** Hi, I'm Bob. And what's 11 ______ name?
**MARIA** 12 ______ name is Maria.
**BOB** Hi, Maria. 13 ______ to meet 14 ______.

**GRAMMAR**
Questions

**2** **Match the pictures and write the conversations.**

Are you from Brazil?

1 *– What's your name?*
*– Carla.*

2 ______________________
______________________

3 ______________________
______________________

4 ______________________
______________________

**VOCABULARY**
Flats and houses

**3** Look at the photos. Choose the best words.

We [1]have / live [2]a house / an apartment in Toronto, Canada. It's very [3]big / small, only two rooms and a kitchen.

This is a picture of our [4]house / flat in London. It's a [5]big / small [6]house / flat – six rooms and a kitchen.

I [7]have / live near Moscow, in Russia. This is my [8]house / flat. It's very [9]big / small, but it's nice.

**VOCABULARY**
Numbers 0–10

**4 a** Look at the examples. Write the answers.

1 one + five = *six*.
2 seven – three = *four*.
3 two + three = ______.
4 three + six + one = ______.
5 five – four = ______.
6 eight + one = ______.
7 five + four – one = ______.
8 ten – three = ______.

**b** What is the next number? Write the word.

a 1, 2, 3, 4 … *five*
b 2, 4, 6 … ______
c 1, 3, 5 … ______
d 10, 9, 8, 7, … ______
e 3, 6 … ______
f 10, 7, 4 … ______

**VOCABULARY**
*boy, girl …*

**5** Look at the picture. Find:

1 a father and a child *H*
2 a small boy in a car ______
3 two mothers ______
4 five girls ______
5 a very small car ______
6 a mother and two children ______

**GRAMMAR**
Questions and answers

**Over to you**
You talk to Li. Look at questions 1–4. Write *your* answers!

**6** Li is at a party. What are his questions?

1 name? *What's your name?*
2 where from? ______
3 married? ______
4 student? ______

# TimeOut

**7** Write words in the crossword.

ACROSS (→)
1 Barack Obama is from the ______.
3 We live in a small ______ in London.
5 This is our ______. (see photo A)
7 I'm from Costa Rica, but I ______ in Miami.
8 This is my ______. (see picture B)
10 We have three ______, a girl and two boys.

DOWN (↓)
2 I live in England. I have an ______ in London.
3 A How are you?
B I'm ______ thanks.
4 This is my ______. (see photo B)
6 I have three children, two ______ and a boy.
9 Hi! I'm Li Yong. I'm from Shanghai. It's a town in ______.

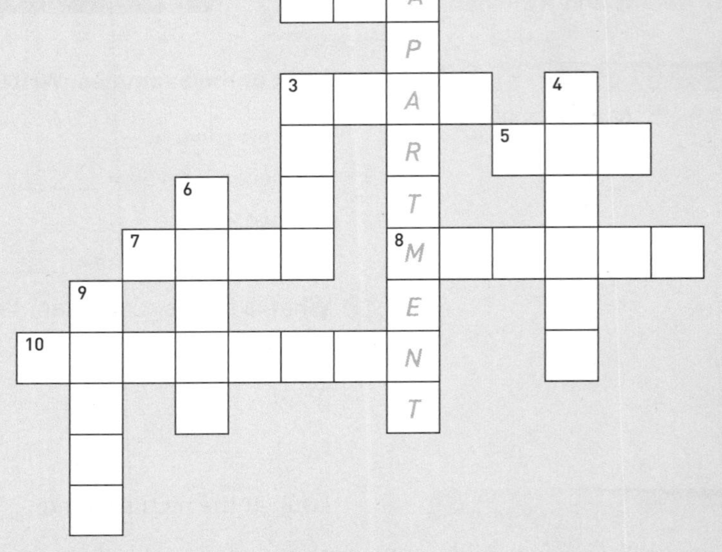


A

B

# EXPLORE Writing

| Small letters | Capital (= big) letters |
|---|---|
| a, b, c, d ... | A, B, C, D ... |

8 a We use capital letters for:

| | ☺ | ☹ Not ... |
|---|---|---|
| **the word 'I'.** | **I**'m a student. | ~~i'm a student.~~ |
| **the start of a sentence.** | **T**his is my car. | ~~this is my car.~~ |
| **names.** | I'm **O**mar **F**arid.<br>My car is a **F**iat. | ~~I'm omar farid.~~<br>~~My car is a fiat.~~ |
| **towns and countries.** | I live in **T**okyo.<br>I'm from **R**ussia. | ~~I live in tokyo.~~<br>~~I'm from russia.~~ |

**Look at these words. Which words have capital letters? Write them correctly.**

1 hitachi *Hitachi*
2 student ✓
3 the usa ______
4 photo ______
5 china ______
6 paris ______
7 barack obama ______
8 car ______
9 you ______
10 brazil ______
11 toyota ______
12 new york ______

b **Write these sentences correctly. Add capital letters.**

1 i'm from oxford. it's a town in england. where are you from?

______

2 hi! my name is brigitte neumann. i'm a student in berlin.

______

3 my mother lives in london, but i live in australia.

______

4 we have two children, a girl and a boy.

______

**Writing reference and practice, Punctuation, p54 Capitals (1), p55**

# DVD-ROM Extra Nice to meet you

1 **Before you watch, look at the maps.**

2 **Watch the video. Who is:**

- Wai Kee?
- Katie?
- Paula?

3 **Who says these things?**

1 Thank you. *Wai Kee*
2 How are you? ___________
3 Fine, thanks. ___________
4 This is Paula. ___________
5 What's your name? ___________

4 **Watch Wai Kee again. Complete the sentences.**

1 I study ___________.
2 I'm from ___________.

5 **Watch Paula again. Circle the correct answers.**

1 I'm from (Ireland) / Manchester.
2 We live in Ireland / Manchester.
3 I'm married / not married.
4 I have no children / two children.
5 We live in a small flat / house near the university.

6 **Watch Katie again. Complete the sentences. Use expressions from the box.**

on campus near London a small town with the other students

1 Hatfield is ___________.
2 I live ___________.

7 **Watch the last part again. Complete the sentences.**

KATIE OK, well, 1___________, Paula.
PAULA Yes, 2___________.
WAI KEE 3___________, Katie.

# 2 People

VOCABULARY
Family

**1 Write words in the gaps.**

~~husband~~ sister daughter father brother children son mother

The Catalano family, 1985

1 wife and *husband*

2 ____________ and ____________

3 ____________ and ____________

4 ____________ and ____________

5 *parents* and ____________

VOCABULARY
Numbers 1–20

**2 a Write two more numbers.**

1 one, two, *three*, *four*
2 two, four, ________, ________
3 three, six, ________, ________
4 seven, eight, ________, ________
5 twelve, thirteen, ________, ________
6 five, ten, ________, ________
7 twenty, nineteen, ________, ________
8 ten, nine, ________, ________

**b Write numbers as words in the gaps.**

1 Julie is *thirteen*.
2 He lives at ____________ New Street.
3 You're in room ____________.
4 The phone is ____________ dollars.
5 The box is ____________ kilos.
6 The Catalano family have ____________ children.

**GRAMMAR**
*He's ..., She's ...*

**3** **Look at the photos. Which country? Write sentences.**

- He's from ...
- She's from ...
- They're from ...

1 China? the USA?

2 England? the USA?

3 China? Germany?

4 Vietnam? the USA?

5 England? Brazil?

6 Japan? Russia?

1 *She's from China.* ______
2 ______
3 ______
4 ______
5 ______
6 ______

**VOCABULARY**
Work

**4** **a** **Write the words in two lists.**

~~waiter~~ ~~supermarket~~ hospital café school manager shop teacher doctor restaurant office student hotel university bank

| People | Places |
|---|---|
| *waiter* | *supermarket* |
| ______ | ______ |
| ______ | ______ |
| ______ | ______ |
| ______ | ______ |
| | ______ |
| | ______ |
| | ______ |
| | ______ |
| | ______ |

**b** Write words from 4a in the puzzle. They are all people or places.

1 He works in a school. He's a ... .
2 See picture A. Jolly's is a book ... .
3 I'm a ... . I study English.
4 See picture B.
5 She's a manager. She works in the New York ... .
6 He's a ... . He works in a restaurant.
7 See picture C.
8 See picture D.
9 She's a doctor. She works in a ... .

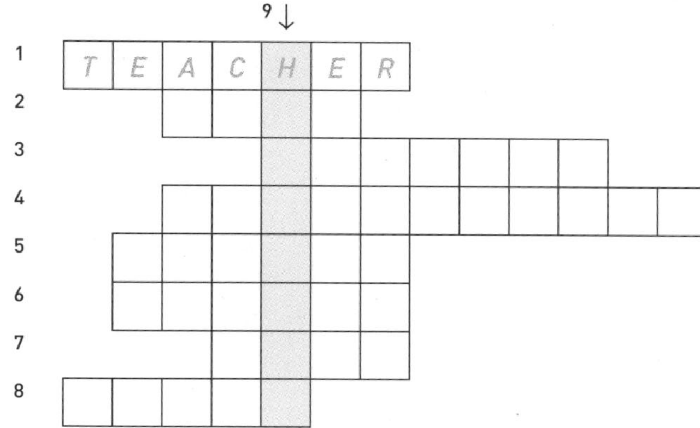

**GRAMMAR**
*He / She works*

**5 a** Complete the table.

| | |
|---|---|
| I am (I'm) | He / She [1] *is* |
| I live | He / She [2] ______ |
| I work | He / She [3] ______ |
| I have | He / She [4] ______ |

**b** Anita answers questions in the street. Read her answers. Add verbs.

**Questionnaire**

Name: *Anita Patel*
Age: 20–25 ☐ 26–30 ☑ 30+ ☐
Married? Yes ☑ No ☐
Children? 0 ☑ 1 ☐ 2 ☐ 3+ ☐
Home: room ☐ house ☐ flat ☑
Where? *Camden, London*
Job: *doctor – hospital*

[1] I *'m* 27.
[2] I ______ married, but I ______ no children.
[3] I ______ in London. I ______ a flat in Camden.
[4] I ______ a doctor.
[5] I ______ in a hospital.

**Over to you**

Answer the questionnaire for *you*.
Then write three true sentences.
- I'm ...
- I live ...
- I work ...
- I have ...

**c** Read the sentences about Anita. Add verbs.

Anita [1] *is* 27. She [2] ______ married but she [3] ______ no children. She [4] ______ in London. She [5] ______ a doctor and she [6] ______ in a hospital. She [7] ______ a small flat near the hospital.

# EXPLORE Reading

6 a Donna is at the Eden Plaza Hotel in London. Look at her passport and the hotel form.

CANADA
Type P
Issuing country CDN
Passport number 09519636
Surname WYATT
Given names DONNA
Nationality CANADIAN
Date of birth 12.02.1976
Date of issue 01.09.2009
Date of expiry 01.09.2019
P<WYATT<<DONNA<<<<<<<<<<<<<<<<<<<<<<<<<<<<<<<<<<
09519636<<<<<<<<<<<<<<<<<<<<<<<<<<<<<<<<<<<<<<<



**Eden Plaza, Newcastle**

**Visitor's registration form**

| Family name | First name(s) | |
|---|---|---|
| Wyatt | Donna | |
| Address: 16 Barton road, London BR11 6LM, England | | |
| Phone no.: 098 65732 | Date of birth: 12.02.1976 | |
| Nationality: Canadian | Occupation: Bank manager | |
| Passport no.: 095 19636 | Date and place of issue: 01.09.2009 Montreal, Canada | |
| Arrival date: 12.05.2010 | Departure date: 14.05.2010 | Room no.: 613 |

b Correct the sentences.

1 Her first name is Wyatt. *Her first name is Donna.*
2 She is from the USA. ______
3 She lives in Canada. ______
4 She is a teacher. ______
5 The hotel is in London. ______
6 She is at the hotel for four nights. ______
7 She is in room 16. ______

7 **Write these words in your language. Guess, or use a dictionary.**

first name = ______
family name (or last name) = ______
address = ______
phone number = ______
nationality = ______
occupation = ______
date of birth = ______
passport = ______

no. = number

8 **You are at the Eden Plaza Hotel for seven nights. Complete the form.**

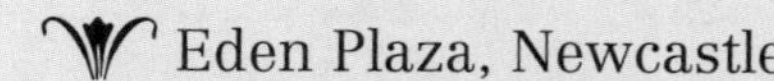
**Eden Plaza, Newcastle**

**Visitor's registration form**

| Family name | First name(s) | |
|---|---|---|
| Address | | |
| Phone no. | Date of birth | |
| Nationality | Occupation | |
| Passport no. | Date and place of issue | |
| Arrival date | Departure date | Room no. 425 |

1 **Before you watch, think about your family.**

- Is it big or small?
- Do you have brothers and sisters, a husband or wife, children?

2 **Watch the video. Tick (✓) the correct answers.**

**Wai Kee talks about:**
his father ☐
his brother ☐
his mother ☐
his sister ☐

**Paula talks about:**
her father ☐
her brother ☐
her children ☐
her mother ☐
her husband ☐

3 **Watch again and complete the sentences. Use words from the box.**

| ~~Apple~~ a doctor an office the BBC a teacher a hospital a school |
|---|

**Wai Kee**

1 My father works for *Apple*.
2 My mother is ____________.
3 She works in ____________.

**Paula**

1 My father works in ____________.
2 He's ____________.
3 My husband works in ____________.
4 He works for ____________.

4 **Who is in the family photos?**

| ~~husband~~ mother sister son daughter |
|---|

**Paula's photos**

*husband*
____________
____________

**Wai Kee's photos**

____________
____________

5 **Circle the correct answers.**

1 How old are Paula's children?
a five and nine
b seven and nine
c 12 and nine

2 How old is Wai Kee's sister?
a five
b nine
c 19

3 Where is Wai Kee's job?
a in a shop
b in a restaurant
c in a café

# 3 Where and when?

A Taormina, Italy

B Tokyo, Japan

**GRAMMAR**
*there's / there are*

**1** **Look at the photos. Write *There's* or *There are* in the gaps.**

1 *There are* cars and buses in the street. [B]
2 *There's* a big mosque. [–]
3 ________ old houses. [ ]
4 ________ a cinema. [ ]
5 ________ an old church. [ ]
6 ________ a restaurant. [ ]
7 ________ lots of offices. [ ]
8 ________ people, but no cars. [ ]

**VOCABULARY**
Streets

**2** **a** **Which photo? Write A, B or – beside the sentences.**

**b** **Which sentences are true? Write *Yes* or *No*.**

**photo A**
1 It's a beautiful street. ______
2 It's a quiet street. ______
3 It's a busy street. ______

**photo B**
1 It's a beautiful street. ______
2 It's a busy street. ______
3 It's a noisy street. ______

**VOCABULARY**
Places in towns

**3** **a** **Find the places on the map. Write letters.**

1 We're at the Olympia Restaurant. It's in New Street, near the cinema. [ ]
2 We're in Old Street, near the Plaza Hotel. We're in a bookshop. [ ]
3 I'm at the Star Supermarket. It's next to the Adelphi Cinema. [ ]
4 I'm in a small café just next to the Plaza Hotel. [ ]

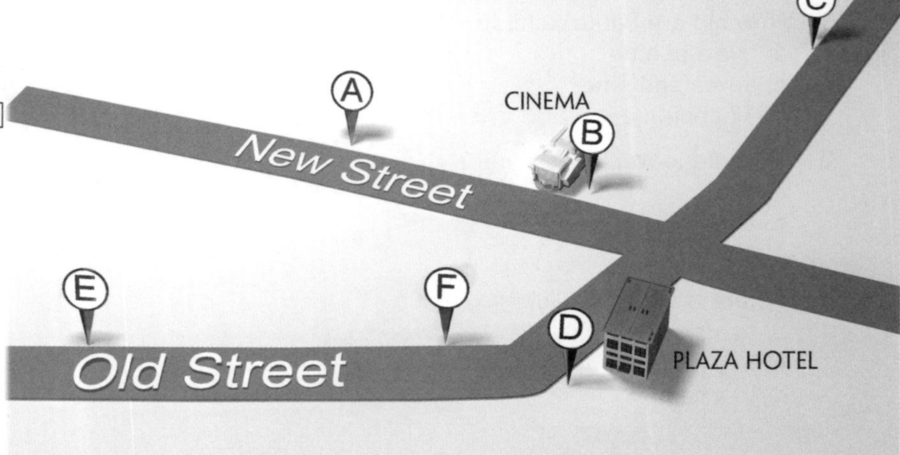

**b** **Put the conversation in order. Write numbers.**

A Hi. It's me. *1*
B OK. See you there. ___
A It's in Market Street. ___
B Where's that? ___
B Hi. Where are you? ___
A I'm at the bus station. ___

**VOCABULARY**
Clock times

**4 a Write the times.**

a 5.15 *five fifteen*
b 2.45 ______
c 12.20 ______
d 10.00 ______
e 6.30 ______
f 3.00 ______

**b Write these times. Use *about*.**

1 *It's about six thirty.* 2 ______ 3 ______

**VOCABULARY**
Days

**5 a Write the days.**

1 **unSday** *Sunday*
2 **shruTday** ______
3 **donMay** ______
4 **irdyaF** ______
5 **sueyadT** ______
6 **urdaStay** ______
7 **nedWesday** ______

**b Complete the sentences.**

OPEN
11.00 a.m. – 12.00 p.m.
Closed Mon

1 There's a boat to Naxos *on Monday and Thursday* ______.
2 The office is open ______.
3 ______, the supermarket is open from 9 a.m. to 4 p.m.
4 There is no bus on ______ or ______.
5 The restaurant is closed ______.

VOCABULARY
*in, on, at*

6 a Circle the correct preposition.

1 I'm free in / on Wednesday afternoon. T
2 I'm in London in / on Thursday and Friday. ☐
3 I'm at work in / on Monday, but I'm free in / on the afternoon. ☐
4 I'm at home on / at 5.30 on / at Friday. ☐
5 I'm not free on / at Saturday evening. ☐
6 My birthday is in / on Tuesday. ☐

b Look at Paul's diary. Are sentences 1–6 true or false? Write T or F.

Paul

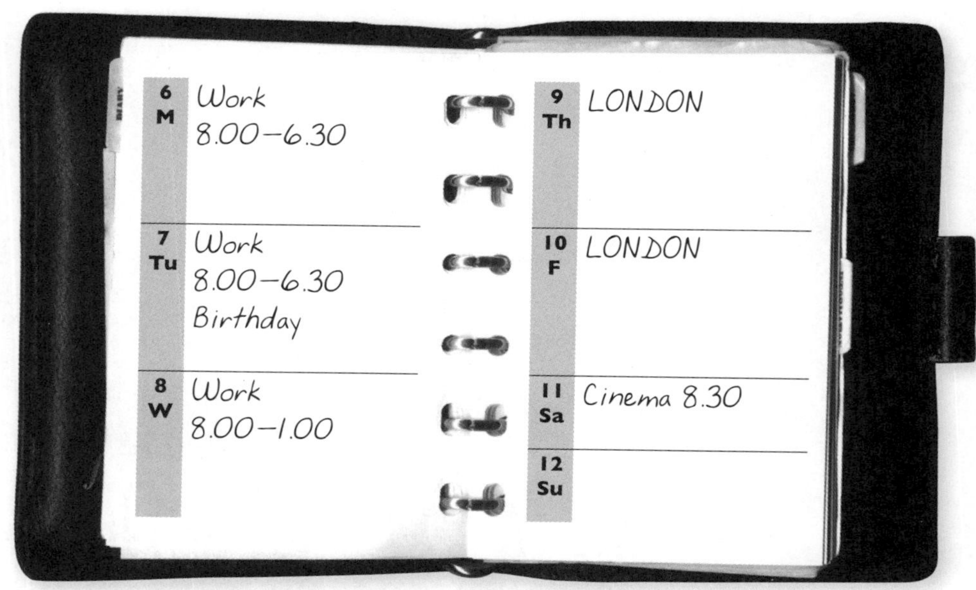


VOCABULARY
*Let's meet ...*

7 Paul wants to meet a friend in London. What does he say?

PAUL [1]meet / coffee / for / Let's / .
SALMA OK. When are you free?
PAUL [2]you / Thursday / free / Are / morning / on / ?
SALMA Yes, I think so.
PAUL [3]meet / Let's / 10.30 / the café / at / at / .
SALMA OK. See you there.

1 ______________________________
2 ______________________________
3 ______________________________

**Over to you**

You want to meet a friend. Choose a time and a place. Write three sentences like Paul's.

# TimeOut

8 Look at the pictures. Find seven words in the word square. They go across (→) and down (↓).

| O | C | A | R | O | P |
|---|---|---|---|---|---|
| S | H | O | U | S | E |
| B | U | S | I | H | O |
| T | R | E | E | O | P |
| U | C | A | F | P | L |
| X | H | O | U | A | E |

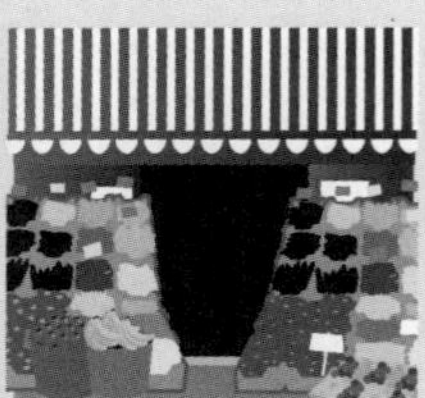

# EXPLORE Writing

**These are pronouns:**
*I, we, you, he, she, it, they*

9 a **We can use pronouns to join ideas.**

| | | |
|---|---|---|
| My brother works for Bank of Saudi Arabia.<br>My brother lives in Dubai. | → | My brother works for Bank of Saudi Arabia.<br>**He** lives in Dubai.<br>(*he = my brother*) |
| Anna is a teacher.<br>Anna teaches English. | → | Anna is a teacher.<br>**She** teaches English.<br>(*she = Anna*) |
| I'm a student in Bristol.<br>Bristol is a nice place to study. | → | I'm a student in Bristol.<br>**It**'s a nice place to study.<br>(*it = Bristol*) |
| We have two children.<br>The children are both at school. | → | We have two children.<br>**They** are both at school.<br>(*they = the children*) |

**Change the words in bold to pronouns.**

1 This is my friend Kim. **Kim** is from Korea. ___*She*___
2 My parents are over 80. **My parents** live in Buenos Aires. ____________
3 We live in Naples. **Naples** is a town in Florida. ____________
4 Paula is 20. **Paula** is a student in Berlin. ____________
5 I have a new car. **The car** is a Toyota. ____________

b **We can use *and* to join ideas.**

| | | |
|---|---|---|
| They're married.<br>They have two children.<br>(*two sentences*) | → | They're married and they have two children.<br>(*one sentence*) |

**Look at the notes. Write *four* sentences. Use pronouns and *and*.**

my sister
Australia
married
two children
both girls
Amy – six
Vanessa – three

*My sister lives in Australia.*
______________________________
______________________________
______________________________

# 3 DVD-ROM Extra Let's meet for a coffee

1 **Before you watch, think about shops.**

- Are there food shops in your street?
- When are they open?

2 **Watch the first part of the video. Answer the questions.**

1 What's the time? ______________________

2 Is the shop open or closed? ______________________

3 Where is a shop open? ______________________

4 When is it open? ______________________

3 **Watch the next part. Circle the correct answers.**

Paula and Giacomo arrange to meet:

1 a tomorrow.
  b on Wednesday.
  c on Thursday.

2 a at the university.
  b at a café.
  c at the theatre.

3 a at 2 o'clock.
  b at 3 o'clock.
  c at 4 o'clock.

4 **Where is Shaun's Café? Find it on the map.**

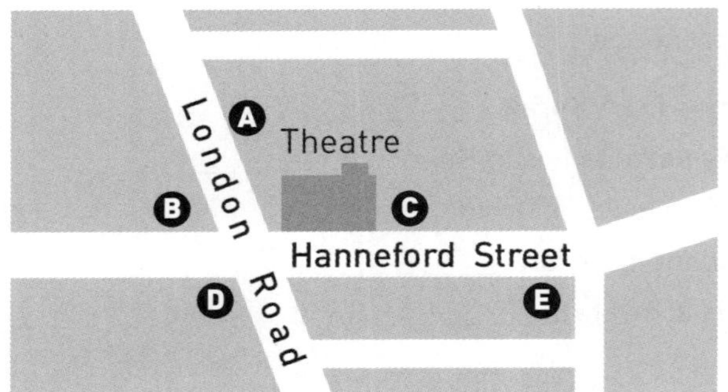


5 **Watch again. Complete what Paula says.**

1 *Are you* ______________ tomorrow? ______________ for coffee.

2 OK, ______________ on Thursday afternoon.

3 ______________ Shaun's Café?

6 **You talk to Giacomo. Write a conversation.**

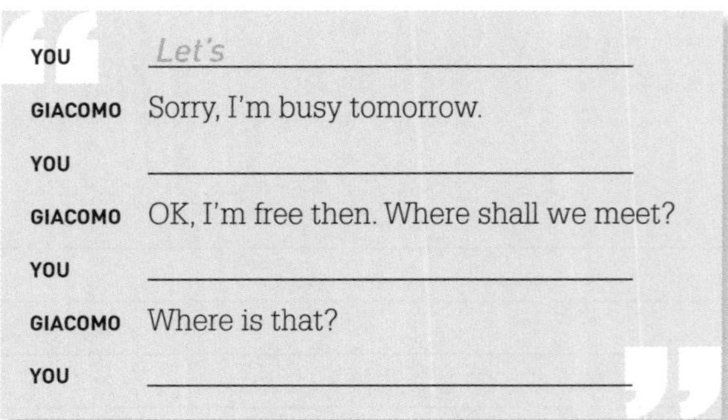

YOU *Let's* ______________________

GIACOMO Sorry, I'm busy tomorrow.

YOU ______________________

GIACOMO OK, I'm free then. Where shall we meet?

YOU ______________________

GIACOMO Where is that?

YOU ______________________

4

# About you

VOCABULARY
Activity verbs

1 a Match the verbs and nouns.

1 watch
2 listen
3 read
4 speak
5 go
6 have
7 live

a to university
b TV
c Spanish
d to the radio
e books
f in Mexico City
g two brothers

b Write the verbs and nouns from 1a in the gaps.

**Conchita talks about her life as a student in Tampico, in Mexico.**

**University** I [1] *go* [2] ____________ in Tampico. It's a big town in Mexico, about 200 kilometres from Mexico City.

**Family** I [3] ____________ [4] ____________. They're both married and they [5] ____________ [6] ____________.

**Languages** Well, I'm from Mexico, so of course I [7] ____________ [8] ____________. I also speak English and a bit of French.

**Books and magazines** I study English, so I [9] ____________ [10] ____________ in English, and in Spanish. I don't read magazines much – I don't have time.

**Radio and TV** I don't [11] ____________ [12] ____________ much, but I [13] ____________ [14] ____________ a lot – I have a small radio in my room.

GRAMMAR
*I don't ...*

2 Match 1–5 with a–b and write the sentences.

1 I don't play sport
2 I speak English and French
3 I play tennis
4 I don't play the guitar
5 I don't often go to the cinema

a but I don't play basketball.
b but I watch a lot of DVDs.
c but I watch it on TV.
d but I don't speak Russian.
e but I love guitar music.

1 ____________
2 ____________
3 ____________
4 ____________
5 ____________

VOCABULARY
Food and drink

3 Find eight words for food and drink. Write them under the pictures.

meatfruitvegetablescoffeebreadpastawaterrice

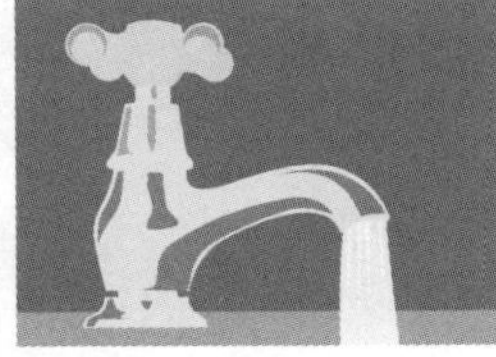
1 ____________

2 ____________

3 ____________

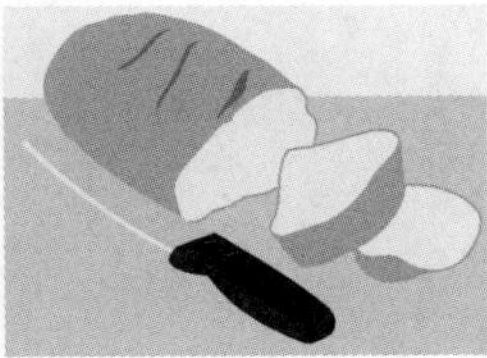
4 ____________

5 ____________

6 ____________

7 ____________

8 ____________

**VOCABULARY**
*often, sometimes ...*

**4** **Add a word from the box to the sentences so they are true for you.**

| often | sometimes | never |
|---|---|---|

1 I __________ watch sport on TV.
2 I __________ listen to the radio in the morning.
3 I __________ eat rice.
4 I __________ drink coffee in the evening.
5 I __________ sleep in the afternoon.
6 I __________ get up before 7.00.

**VOCABULARY**
Countries and nationalities

**5** **a** **Complete the table.**

| | |
|---|---|
| England | 1 *English* |
| France | 2 *French* |
| the USA | 3 *American* |
| Spain | 4 __________ |
| Italy | 5 __________ |
| China | 6 __________ |
| Russia | 7 __________ |
| Japan | 8 __________ |
| India | 9 __________ |

**b** **The words in bold are wrong . Write them correctly.**

1 We often eat in an **Italy** restaurant. __________
2 Sorry, I don't speak **Japan**. __________
3 She's from **Russian**. She lives in St Petersburg. __________
4 I love **China** food. __________
5 We're from Bangalore. It's a city in **Indian**. __________

**VOCABULARY**
Adjectives

**6** **Read about the two cafés. Choose the best adjective.**

Café Roma is in the market area, near the city centre, so it's always [1]quiet / busy. It's a very [2]small / big café, with only five tables. The coffee is good and it's very [3]cheap / expensive.

Café Rimbaud is in a [4]quiet / noisy street near the theatre. It's a [5]small / big café, with about 30 tables and a garden. The coffee is good, but it's very [6]cheap / expensive.

GRAMMAR
*Do you ...?*

7 a Complete the table.

| ⊕ | ❓ |
|---|---|
| I live ... | 1 *Do you live* ...? |
| I work ... | 2 ______ ...? |
| I have ... | 3 ______ ...? |

b Read the interview and complete the questions.

INTERVIEWER [1]______ ______ ______ children?
ANITA No. I'm married, but I don't have children.
INTERVIEWER [2]______ ______ ______ coffee in the morning?
ANITA No, tea, usually.
INTERVIEWER [3]______ ______ ______ a newspaper?
ANITA Yes, an evening paper, sometimes.
INTERVIEWER [4]______ ______ ______ meat?
ANITA No, only vegetables – and fish sometimes.
INTERVIEWER [5]______ ______ ______ a car?
ANITA Yes, a Peugeot.
INTERVIEWER [6]______ ______ ______ to the radio?
ANITA Yes, when I'm in the car. But not at home.

c Look at Anita's answers. Complete the questionnaire.

**Over to you**

Answer the questionnaire for you. Then choose three questions. Write answers.
*I have a car. It's a Toyota.*

**Questionnaire**

**Name:** *Anita Patel*
**Married?** Yes ☐ No ☐
**Children?** 0 ☐ 1 ☐ 2 ☐ 3+ ☐
**Morning?** coffee ☐ tea ☐
**Newspaper?** morning ☐ evening ☐
**Meat?** Yes ☐ No ☐
**Car?** Yes ☐ (What?) ______ No ☐
**Radio?** Yes ☐ No ☐

# EXPLORE Reading

8 **Look at the advertisements. Which one is for:**

1 a hotel? ______
2 an apartment? ______
3 a school? ______
4 a café? ______
5 a restaurant? ______

**A**

Quiet apartment in city centre.
3 rooms, kitchen.
€250 a month.
Phone 657 4933.

**B**

Learn to SPEAK ENGLISH

Lingua School of English
✓ small classes (8–12 students)
✓ all teachers are from Britain and the USA

**C**

EXCELSIOR INTERNATIONAL
★★★★
• comfortable rooms with TV
• business centre
• two restaurants
• fitness centre
• near the airport

**D**

NEW SAIGON
Business lunch 12 – 2 p.m. only £15
Vietnamese and international food

**E**

COPACABANA café and bar
open 11.a.m.–11. p.m.
Live Brazilian music Fri and Sat

9 **People talk about the five places. Find two things that are *different* in the advertisements.**

**A** It's a very small flat. And it's in the centre, so it's noisy.

*It's a big flat (three rooms).*
*It's quiet.*

**B** I go to the Lingua School. It's not very good. The classes are big and the teachers don't speak good English.

______
______

**C** I like the Excelsior. It's in the city centre. Only one problem – there's no restaurant in the hotel.

______
______

**D** The New Saigon is a good Chinese restaurant and it's cheap. Lunch is only £10.

______
______

**E** There's a new café in our street – the Cobacabana. It's open in the morning, but it closes at eight in the evening. They have live music on Saturday and Sunday.

______
______

10 **Use a dictionary. Find the words in bold.**

1 €250 a **month**
2 **live** music
3 **comfortable** rooms
4 **fitness** centre
5 business **lunch**
6 **international** food

1 **Before you watch, think about cafés.**

- Do you often go to cafés?
- What do you often have? Tea, coffee, water, cola ...?

2 **Watch the video. What do they ask for? Tick (✓) the drinks.**

milk ☐
espresso ☐
tea ☐
espresso with milk ☐
tea with milk ☐
water ☐

3 **Paula and Giacomo talk about football. Who:**

1 plays football? ___________
2 watches football on TV? ___________
3 goes to football matches? ___________

4 **Paula talks about her family. What do they do on Saturday? Make sentences.**

| | |
|---|---|
| Paula and her husband<br>The children<br>They all | stay at home in the morning.<br>go to a football match.<br>watch TV or a DVD.<br>read the paper.<br>listen to the radio. |

5 **Watch again. Do they say these things? Write *Yes* or *No*.**

1 GIACOMO In Italy, people never drink coffee with milk. _No_
2 PAULA I drink a lot of tea. ______
3 GIACOMO I play football every day. ______
4 PAULA My children don't like football matches. ______
5 GIACOMO I never go to football matches. ______

6 **You ask for something in a café. Write a sentence. Begin:**

- I'll have ...

*or*

- I'd like ...

# 5 Things to buy

VOCABULARY
Common objects

**1 Look at the pictures and write the words in the puzzle.**

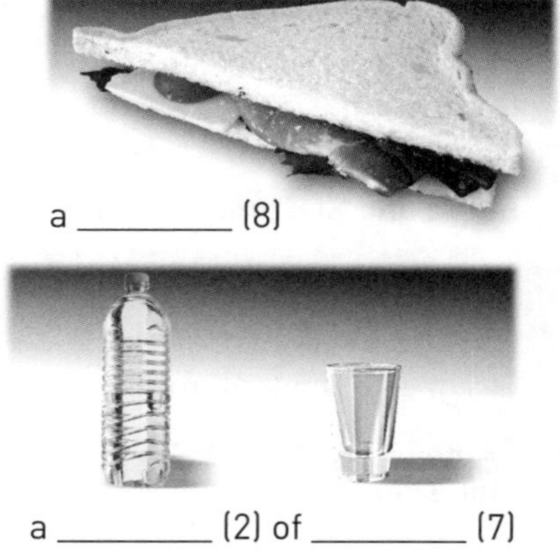

a ________ (8)

a ________ (2) of ________ (7)
and a ________ (6)

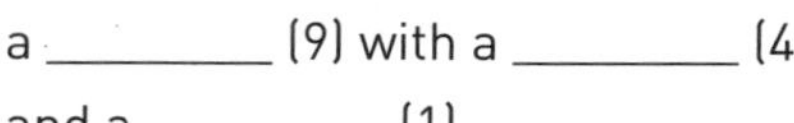

a ________ (9) with a ________ (4),
and a ________ (1)

a ________ (5)

a ________ (3)

GRAMMAR
Singular and plural nouns

**2 a Write plurals.**

1 pen *pens*
2 watch ____________
3 bottle ____________
4 magazine ____________
5 sandwich ____________
6 glass ____________

**b Read the conversation at a kiosk. Complete what A says. Write the words in order.**

A [1] *Do* ____________________? (you / pens / sell / Do)
B No, sorry. We don't.
A [2] ____________________? (water / bottles / have / you / Do / of).
B Yes. Large or small?
A Small, please.

**VOCABULARY**
Clothes

**3 a Look at the picture. Find:**

1 a man with a suit and tie. ___I___
2 a girl with a dress. ______
3 a boy with jeans and a T-shirt. ______
4 a man with jeans and a pullover. ______
5 a woman with a skirt. ______
6 a woman with a coat and a hat. ______
7 a man with a jacket and trousers. ______

**b Choose three other people. Write about them.**

*J a man with trousers and a shirt*
_______________________________________________
_______________________________________________
_______________________________________________

**VOCABULARY**
Numbers, prices

## % SALE %
### FANTASTIC PRICES!

SHIRTS ~~£75~~ £40
TROUSERS ~~£75~~ £45
PULLOVERS ~~£65~~ £25
BAGS ~~£25~~ £10
JEANS ~~£90~~ £30
TIES ~~£15~~ £5
SKIRTS ~~£40~~ £25

**4 Write the prices for these clothes.**

1 Two shirts *eighty pounds*
2 Three pullovers ____________
3 A pair of jeans and a bag ____________
4 A skirt and a pullover ____________
5 A shirt and a tie ____________
6 Two pairs of trousers ____________
7 Three pairs of jeans and a bag ____________

VOCABULARY
Colours

5 **Write the colours correctly.**

- They have a [1]**kacbl** and [2]**hitew** cat.
- The American flag is [3]**der**, [4]**thewi** and [5]**lube**.
- At work, I usually wear a [6]**yerg** or [7]**bworn** suit.
- Brazil's football colours are [8]**nereg**, [9]**elwoyl** and [10]**uble**.

1 ____________ 6 ____________
2 ____________ 7 ____________
3 ____________ 8 ____________
4 ____________ 9 ____________
5 ____________ 10 ____________

GRAMMAR
He / she doesn't, + verb

6 a **Complete the table.**

| **I ...** | **He / She ...** |
|---|---|
| don't like | 1 *doesn't like* |
| don't wear | 2 ____________ |
| don't have | 3 ____________ |
| don't eat | 4 ____________ |

b **Complete the sentences with verbs from the table.**

1 I like red and blue, but I *don't like* yellow.
2 He usually wears a jacket at work, but he ____________ a tie.
3 She eats fish and vegetables, but she ____________ meat.
4 I have one brother, but I ____________ any sisters.
5 My son likes lemonade, but he ____________ cola.

## TimeOut

7 **Look at the market stall. Find nine things in the word square. They go across (→) and down (↓).**

| B | I | C | Y | C | L | E |
|---|---|---|---|---|---|---|
| P | C | A | I | R | A | T |
| L | H | R | P | A | M | E |
| A | A | P | C | U | P | S |
| T | I | E | X | P | O | D |
| E | R | T | B | A | G | S |
| S | S | H | O | E | S | L |

# EXPLORE**Writing**

8 a **Read these sentences about offices in Britain.**

> “In most offices, men wear a suit **and** a tie, **or** a jacket **and** trousers.”

> “Women wear a suit **or** a skirt **or** sometimes trousers, **but** not jeans.”

**Notice how we can join nouns together.**

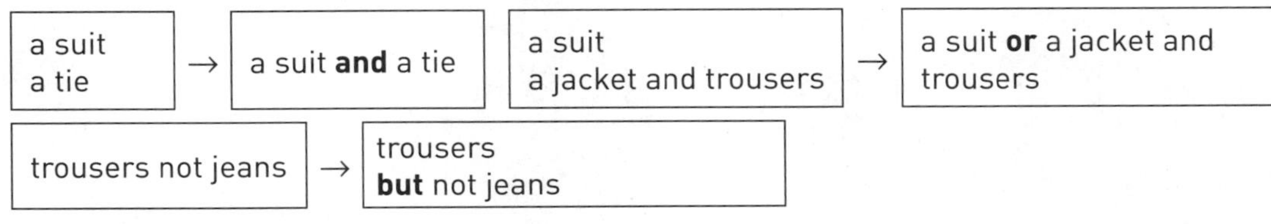

| | | | | | | |
|---|---|---|---|---|---|---|
| a suit<br>a tie | → | a suit **and** a tie | a suit<br>a jacket and trousers | → | a suit **or** a jacket and trousers |
| trousers not jeans | → | trousers<br>**but** not jeans | | | |

**Join these nouns with *and*, *or* or *but*.**

1 At home, I usually wear jeans – a T-shirt – a shirt.

______________________________

2 You can wear a dress – a skirt – not trousers.

______________________________

3 We usually eat fish – vegetables – rice – not meat.

______________________________

4 In the morning I usually drink tea – coffee – a glass of orange juice.

______________________________

b **We can join *sentences* in the same way.**

| | | |
|---|---|---|
| Most men wear a suit **and** women wear a dress or a skirt. | Most men wear a suit at work, **or** they wear a jacket and trousers. | Men often wear a shirt and a tie, **but** they don't usually wear a suit. |

**Write sentences about you. Join the ideas with *and*, *or* or *but*.**

1 At home I usually wear …
2 At work / school, I usually wear …
3 At home, we often eat …
4 In the morning, I usually drink …

# 5 DVD-ROM Extra In a clothes shop

1 **Before you watch, look at the photo.**

- Where are they?
- What clothes can you see?

2 **Watch the video. Circle the correct words.**

1 Katie likes / doesn't like the blue T-shirt.
2 She likes / doesn't like bright colours.
3 She likes / doesn't like the red T-shirt.
4 They only have the red T-shirt in large / small.
5 The jeans are too small / expensive.

3 **What do they say? Match photos A–F with sentences 1–6.**

1 Sorry, we don't have it in small. ___C___
2 Excuse me – how much is this pair of jeans? ______
3 Do you have this in a smaller size? ______
4 I like this T-shirt. ______
5 Oh, sorry! ______
6 What about red? ______

A

B
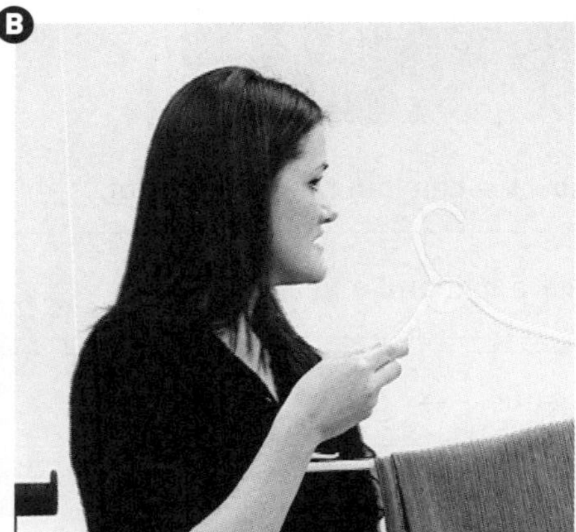

C

D

E

F

4 **Watch again. What does Yolanda wear at work? Tick (✓) the correct words.**

jeans ☐ trousers ☐ a skirt ☐ black clothes ☐ grey clothes ☐ bright colours ☐

5 **Ask about something in the shop. Write three questions.**

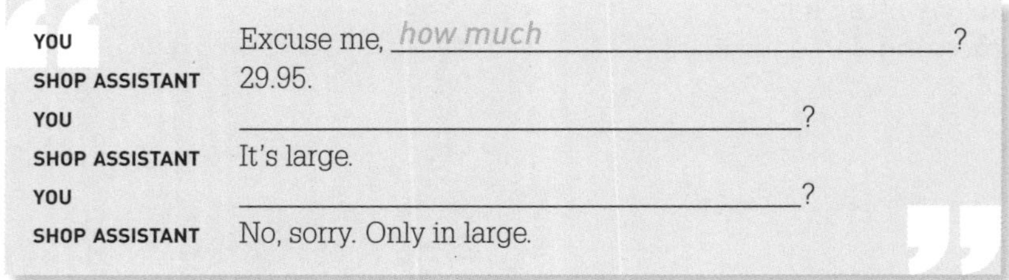

| | |
|---|---|
| **YOU** | Excuse me, *how much* ______________________? |
| **SHOP ASSISTANT** | 29.95. |
| **YOU** | ______________________? |
| **SHOP ASSISTANT** | It's large. |
| **YOU** | ______________________? |
| **SHOP ASSISTANT** | No, sorry. Only in large. |

# 6 Every day

VOCABULARY
Daily routine

1 a Add verbs in the gaps.

have go to come get

1 *go to* school
2 ____________ work
3 ____________ a shower
4 ____________ coffee
5 ____________ home
6 ____________ bed
7 ____________ breakfast
8 ____________ up
9 ____________ lunch

b Read about Hana. Circle the best words.

## Working life

**Hana, a factory worker, talks about her day.**

I [1]start / finish work at seven, so I [2]get up / go to bed at six, [3]have / go a quick breakfast and [4]have / go to work. My husband and our two children [5]get up / go to bed a bit later. They have [6]breakfast / lunch together, then the children go to [7]school / work.

I [8]work / sleep until 10.30, then I have [9]lunch / coffee and a sandwich and read [10]the paper / a book. Then I [11]work / sleep again until one.

The children [12]start / finish school at 1.30, so I meet them at school and we come home and have [13]breakfast / lunch together.

My husband works in an office, so he [14]starts / finishes work at five. We all have [15]lunch / dinner together at about 6.30, then we usually [16]work / watch TV for a bit.

I always [17]get up / go to bed early, usually at about 10 o'clock.

c Answer these questions.

1 Who gets up first? *Hana*
2 Who has breakfast with the children? ____________
3 Who works in an office? ____________
4 Who works in the morning? ____________
5 Who works in the afternoon? ____________
6 Who has lunch at home? ____________

VOCABULARY
Transport

2 a What are the six kinds of transport?

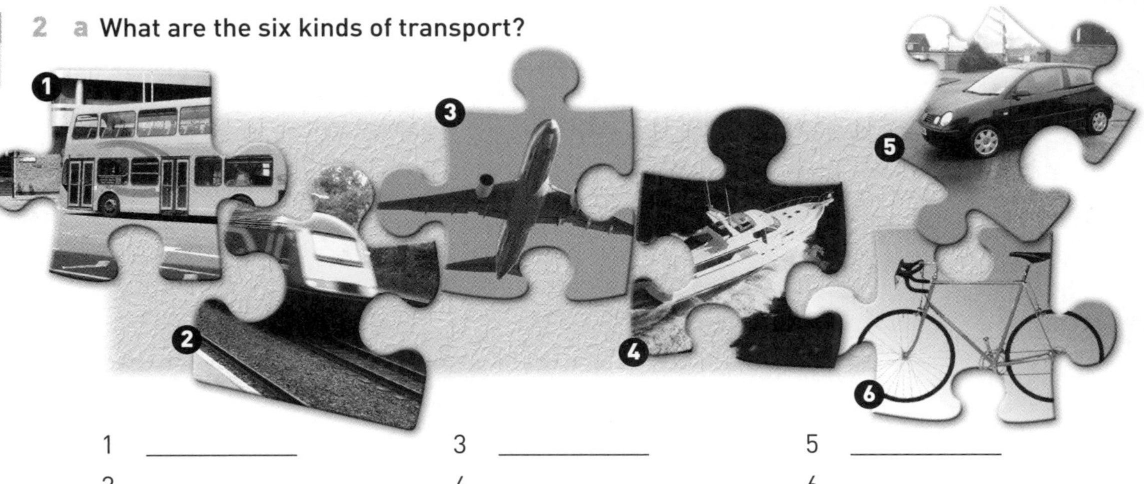

1 ____________
2 ____________
3 ____________
4 ____________
5 ____________
6 ____________

Venice

**b** **Complete the sentences. Use words from the box.**

| ~~by bus~~ | by plane | drive | cycle | by train | by boat | walk |
|---|---|---|---|---|---|---|

1 We always go to school *by bus* .

2 I usually ________ to work, but in bad weather I ________ .

3 I always ________ to work.

4 You can go from London to Glasgow ________ , or you can go ________ .

5 In Venice, you can go everywhere ________ .

VOCABULARY
*How can I get to ... ?*

**3 a** **Put the conversation in order. Write numbers.**

A How much is the bus? ☐
B They're about $45–$50. ☐
A OK, thank you. ☐
B There are buses from the city centre, or you can go by taxi. ☐
A What about taxis? ☐
A Excuse me, how can I get to the airport? *1*
B It's $9.50. ☐

**b** **Write these sentences and questions correctly.**

1 can / go / underground / by / You / there / .
*You can* ________

2 I / How / get / the Sheraton Hotel / can / to / ?
________

3 the airport / How / a taxi / to / much / is / ?
________

4 bus / by / I / Can / there / go / ?
________

VOCABULARY
Adjectives

**4 a** **Find adjectives in the word snake and write them in pairs.**

fastexpensivesmallgoodslowcheapquietbadnoisybig

*fast – slow*
________
________
________
________

# Unit 1

1 2 name 3 I'm 4 from 5 I'm 6 I'm 7 from 8 to 9 meet 10 I'm 11 your 12 My 13 Nice 14 you

2 2 Are you from Brazil?
No, I'm from Argentina.
3 Where are you from?
England.
4 Hello, I'm Sophie.
Hi Sophie. Nice to meet you.

3 2 an apartment 3 small 4 flat 5 big 6 flat 7 live 8 house 9 small

4a 3 five 4 ten 5 one 6 nine 7 eight 8 seven

b b eight c seven d six e nine f one

5 2 F 3 A 4 M 5 K 6 G

6 2 Where are you from? 3 Are you married?
4 Are you a student?

7 **ACROSS (→)** 1 USA 3 flat 5 car 7 live 8 mother 10 children
**DOWN (↓)** 3 fine 4 father 6 girls 9 China

8a 3 the USA 4 ✓ 5 China 6 Paris 7 Barack Obama 8 ✓ 9 ✓ 10 Brazil 11 Toyota 12 New York

b 1 I'm from Oxford. It's a town in England. Where are you from?
2 Hi! My name is Brigitte Neumann. I'm a student in Berlin.
3 My mother lives in London, but I live in Australia.
4 We have two children, a girl and a boy.

## 1 DVD-ROM Extra

2 1 Paula 2 Wai Kee 3 Katie

3 2 Katie 3 Wai Kee 4 Wai Kee 5 Paula

4 1 English 2 Hong Kong

5 1 Ireland 2 Manchester 3 married 4 two children 5 house

6 1 a small town near London
2 on campus with the other students

7 1 nice to meet you 2 goodbye 3 See you

# Unit 2

1 2 father; son 3 mother; daughter 4 sister; brother 5 children

2a 2 six, eight 3 nine, twelve 4 nine, ten 5 fourteen, fifteen 6 fifteen, twenty 7 eighteen, seventeen 8 eight, seven

b 2 seventeen 3 twelve 4 fourteen 5 twenty 6 two

3 2 She's from England. 3 He's from China.
4 She's from the USA. 5 They're from England.
6 She's from Russia.

4 a **People** manager, teacher, doctor, student
**Places** hospital, café, school, shop, restaurant, office, hotel, university, bank

b

| | | | | | 9↓ | | | | | | | | |
|---|---|---|---|---|---|---|---|---|---|---|---|---|---|
| 1 | T | E | A | C | H | E | R | | | | | | |
| 2 | | | S | H | O | P | | | | | | | |
| 3 | | | | | S | T | U | D | E | N | T | | |
| 4 | | | S | U | P | E | R | M | A | R | K | E | T |
| 5 | | O | F | F | I | C | E | | | | | | |
| 6 | | W | A | I | T | E | R | | | | | | |
| 7 | | | | C | A | F | É | | | | | | |
| 8 | H | O | T | E | L | | | | | | | | |

5a 2 lives 3 works 4 has

b 2 'm; have 3 live; have 4 'm 5 work

c 2 is 3 has 4 lives 5 is 6 works 7 has

6b 2 She is from Canada. 3 She lives in England.
4 She is a bank manager.
5 The hotel is in Newcastle.
6 She is at the hotel for two nights.
7 She is in room 613.

## 2 DVD-ROM Extra

2 Wai Kee talks about his father, his mother and his sister.
Paula talks about her father, her children and her husband.

3 **Wai Kee** 2 a teacher 3 a school
**Paula** 1 a hospital 2 a doctor 3 an office 4 the BBC

4 **Paula's photos** son, daughter
**Wai Kee's photos** sister, mother

5 1 a 2 b 3 c

# Unit 3

1 3 There are 4 There's 5 There's 6 There's 7 There are 8 There are

2a 3 A 4 – 5 A 6 A 7 B 8 A

b **photo A** 1 Yes 2 Yes 3 No
**photo B** 1 No 2 Yes 3 Yes

3a 1 A 2 F 3 B 4 D

b A Hi. It's me.
B Hi. Where are you?
A I'm at the bus station.
B Where's that?
A It's in Market Street.
B OK. See you there.

4a b two forty-five c twelve twenty d ten o'clock e six thirty f three o'clock

b 2 It's about ten o'clock. 3 It's about two fifteen.

5a 2 Thursday 3 Monday 4 Friday 5 Tuesday 6 Saturday 7 Wednesday

b 2 on Friday 3 On Sunday 4 Saturday; Sunday 5 on Monday

6a 2 on 3 on; in 4 at; on 5 on 6 on

b 2 T 3 F 4 F 5 T 6 T

7 1 Let's meet for coffee.
2 Are you free on Thursday morning?
3 Let's meet at the café at 10.30.

8

| | | | | | |
|---|---|---|---|---|---|
| O | C | A | R | O | P |
| S | H | O | U | S | E |
| B | U | S | I | H | O |
| T | R | E | E | O | P |
| U | C | A | F | P | L |
| X | H | O | U | A | E |

9a 2 They 3 It 4 She 5 It

b My sister lives in Australia. She is married and has two children. They are both girls. Amy is six and Vanessa is three.

## 3 DVD-ROM Extra

2 1 It's nearly 7 o'clock. 2 It's closed.
3 Near the station. 4 It's open 24 hours.

3 1 c 2 b 3 c

4 C

5 1 free; Let's meet 2 let's meet 3 How about

# Unit 4

1a 1 b 2 d 3 e 4 c 5 a 6 g 7 f

b 2 to university 3 have 4 two brothers 5 live 6 in Mexico City 7 speak 8 Spanish 9 read 10 books 11 watch 12 TV 13 listen 14 to the radio

2 1 I don't play sport but I watch it on TV.
2 I speak English and French but I don't speak Russian.
3 I play tennis but I don't play basketball.
4 I don't play the guitar but I love guitar music.
5 I don't often go to the cinema but I watch a lot of DVDs.

3 1 water 2 pasta 3 rice 4 bread 5 coffee 6 vegetables 7 meat 8 fruit

5a 4 Spanish 5 Italian 6 Chinese 7 Russian 8 Japanese 9 Indian

b 1 Italian 2 Japanese 3 Russia 4 Chinese 5 India

6 1 busy 2 small 3 cheap 4 quiet 5 big 6 expensive

7a 2 Do you work 3 Do you have

b 1 Do you have 2 Do you have / Do you drink 3 Do you read 4 Do you eat 5 Do you have 6 Do you listen

c **Married:** Yes
**Children:** 0
**Morning:** tea
**Newspaper:** evening
**Meat:** No
**Car:** Yes, Peugeot
**Radio:** Yes

8 1 C 2 A 3 B 4 E 5 D

9 B The classes are small. The teachers are from Britain and the USA.
C It's near the airport. It has two restaurants.
D It's a Vietnamese restaurant. Lunch is £15.
E It closes at 11 in the evening. They have live music on Friday and Saturday.

## 4 DVD-ROM Extra

2 tea with milk; espresso with milk

3 1 Giacomo 2 Paula 3 Paula

4 Paula and her husband read the paper. The children watch TV or a DVD. They all stay at home in the morning. They all go to a football match.

5 2 Yes 3 Yes 4 No 5 Yes

# Unit 5

1

| | | | | | 9↓ | | | | | |
|---|---|---|---|---|---|---|---|---|---|---|
| 1 | | | | | P | E | N | | | |
| 2 | | | | B | O | T | T | L | E | |
| 3 | | N | E | W | S | P | A | P | E | R |
| 4 | | | | S | T | A | M | P | | |
| 5 | | W | A | T | C | H | | | | |
| 6 | | | G | L | A | S | S | | | |
| 7 | W | A | T | E | R | | | | | |
| 8 | | S | A | N | D | W | I | C | H | |

2a 2 watches 3 bottles 4 magazines 5 sandwiches 6 glasses

b 1 Do you sell pens?
2 Do you have bottles of water?

3a 2 G 3 D 4 K 5 C 6 E 7 F

b A – a boy with a T-shirt and a hat
B – a man with a T-shirt and trousers
H – a man with a shirt and tie
L – a woman with jeans and a T-shirt

4 2 seventy-five pounds 3 forty pounds 4 fifty pounds 5 forty-five pounds 6 ninety pounds 7 a hundred pounds

5 1 black 2 white 3 red 4 white 5 blue 6 grey 7 brown 8 green 9 yellow 10 blue

6a 2 doesn't wear 3 doesn't have 4 doesn't eat

b 2 doesn't wear 3 doesn't eat 4 don't have 5 doesn't like

7

| | | | | | | |
|---|---|---|---|---|---|---|
| B | I | C | Y | C | L | E |
| P | C | A | I | R | A | T |
| L | H | R | P | A | M | E |
| A | A | P | C | U | P | S |
| T | I | E | X | P | O | D |
| E | R | T | B | A | G | S |
| S | S | H | O | E | S | L |

**8a** 1 At home, I usually wear jeans and a T-shirt or a shirt.
2 You can wear a dress or a skirt, but not trousers.
3 We usually eat fish or vegetables and rice, but not meat.
4 In the morning I usually drink tea or coffee and a glass of orange juice.

## 5 DVD-ROM Extra

**2** 1 doesn't like 2 likes 3 likes 4 large 5 expensive

**3** 2 E 3 A 4 B 5 F 6 D

**4** skirt; trousers; black clothes; grey clothes

# Unit 6

**1a** 2 go to 3 have 4 have 5 come 6 go to 7 have 8 get 9 have

**b** 2 get up 3 have 4 go to 5 get up 6 breakfast 7 school 8 work 9 coffee 10 the paper 11 work 12 finish 13 lunch 14 finishes 15 dinner 16 watch TV 17 go to bed

**c** 2 Hana's husband 3 Hana's husband 4 Hana and her husband 5 Hana's husband 6 Hana and her children

**2a** 1 bus 2 train 3 plane 4 boat 5 car 6 bicycle

**b** 2 walk; drive 3 cycle 4 by train; by plane 5 by boat

**3a** A Excuse me, how can I get to the airport?
B There are buses from the city centre, or you can go by taxi.
A How much is the bus?
B It's $9.50.
A What about taxis?
B They're about $45–$50.
A OK, thank you.

**b** 1 You can go there by underground.
2 How can I get to the Sheraton Hotel?
3 How much is a taxi to the airport?
4 Can I go there by bus?

**4a** expensive – cheap
small – big
good – bad
quiet – noisy

**b** 2 small 3 quiet 4 expensive 5 cheap 6 fast

**5a** 1 Where 2 When 3 What

**b** 2 What do you do on Saturday?; f
3 How do you go to work?; a
4 What do you do in the evening?; d
5 Where do you live?; b
6 Where do you have lunch?; e

**6b** **Subway** fast; crowded
**Buses** cheap; slow; crowded
**Taxis** cheap
**Bicycle** slow; cheap

**7** 1 F 2 T 3 F 4 F 5 T 6 F

## 6 DVD-ROM Extra

**2** 1 5 a.m. 2 6 a.m. 3 12 hours 4 evening 5 after

**3** have dinner; watch TV; go to bed

**4** 1 Magda 2 by train and bus

**5** 17.28 – 18.58
18.04 – 20.04

**6** 1 get 2 go 3 leaves 4 arrives 5 takes

# Unit 7

**1a** 2 listened 3 watched 5 had 6 got 7 met

**b** 1 had 2 listened 3 got 4 went 5 met 6 had 7 went 8 stayed 9 watched

**2a** 2 were 3 was 4 wasn't 5 weren't 6 were 7 was 8 was 9 were

**b** 2 I was in London at the weekend. It was very interesting.
3 Clara wasn't at the meeting on Monday. She was ill.
4 We were in Barcelona last summer. The city was beautiful, but our hotel wasn't very good.
5 I was at Café Metro yesterday. It was very busy and there were lots of people there.

**3** 2 you 3 was 4 it 5 like 6 were 7 you

**4a** 2 on 3 at 4 at 5 in 6 at

**b** 2 T 3 F 4 T 5 T 6 T

**5** 2 A 3 A 4 B 5 B 6 E 7 D 8 C 9 C

**6** **ACROSS (→)** 2 café 6 short 8 long 10 on 11 book
**DOWN (↓)** 1 interesting 2 cheap 3 film 5 school 7 work 9 good

**7a** 2 It 3 there 4 there 5 there

**b** 1 Nine 2 Four 3 so, and, but, there, it

**c** 1 There was a new James Bond film, so we went to see it.
2 *Titanic* is a very good film, but it is very long.
3 I went to the café at six, but my friends weren't there.
4 In 2005, I lived in London and I met my husband there.

## 7 DVD-ROM Extra

**2** 2 Y 3 W 4 Y 5 W 6 Y, W

**3** 2 expensive 3 wonderful 4 terrible, long, boring

**4** On Saturday, he stayed at home and watched a film.
Yesterday, he met friends and had lunch in a restaurant.

**5** 1 T 2 T 3 F 4 F

## Unit 8

1a 2 didn't see 3 bought 4 didn't eat 5 stayed 6 didn't visit 7 had

c 1 saw / visited 2 didn't see / didn't visit 3 didn't go 4 had 5 didn't go 6 didn't visit /didn't see

1 skiing 2 restaurants 3 camping 4 swimming 5 sightseeing 6 shopping

3 2 Did you stay in a hotel? 3 Did you go sightseeing? 4 Did you go to Central Park?

4a 2 October 3 June 4 September 5 March 6 August 7 months

b 2 September 3 April 4 February 5 November, December

5 wet – dry; summer – winter; hot – cold; sunny

6 2 What did you do in New York?; f 3 What was the weather like?; d 4 When did you go there?; a 5 How did you go there?; b 6 Who did you go with?; e

7 1 B 2 C 3 A

8 1 B 2 A 3 B, C 4 B 5 A 6 B, C 7 A, C

### 8 DVD-ROM Extra

2 2 to Cairo 3 his brother 4 five days 5 a great time 6 do much 7 relaxed

3 2 a 3 b 4 d 5 c

4 1 I did a little sightseeing, but not much. 2 He lives in Cairo. He's a student there. 3 The food was very good. 4 It was interesting to meet people from Cairo.

5 1 When did you go? 2 Who did you go with? 3 Where did you stay?

## Unit 9

1a 2 Can I call you later? 3 Are you busy? 4 I'll call you later.

b 2 Oh, hi Hanna, how are you? 3 I'm fine. Are you busy? 4 Yes, I'm still at work. Is it important? 5 No, never mind. I'll call you this evening. 6 Yes, call me at about 8.00. 7 OK. Bye.

2a 2 having 3 listening 4 cooking 5 going 6 writing 7 eating 8 talking

b 2 He's cooking. 3 They're watching TV. 4 She's eating ice cream. 5 They're talking. 6 He's going to work. 7 She's writing. 8 He's listening to music.

3 2 Are you watching TV? 3 No, I'm reading a book. 4 What are you doing? 5 I'm just having lunch. 6 I'm just going to work.

4 2 11 Tu, film on TV, 8.15 3 19 W, party 4 15 Sa, 16 Su, parents 5 12 W, meeting, 9.00 6 12 W, coffee, 4.30 7 13 Th, cinema

5 **ACROSS (→)** 2 cinema 4 football 5 theatre 6 hotel 7 museum 8 restaurant
**DOWN (↓)** 2 café 3 gallery 6 hostel 7 match

6a 1 which 2 which 3 who 4 which 5 who

b 1 and; who; there; which; but 2 **A** 7; **B** 2

c Last year I went to Madrid and stayed with a friend who teaches English there. She lives next to a restaurant which has very good fish and meat dishes, so we ate there every evening.

### 9 DVD-ROM Extra

2 1 Paula and Simon 2 8.00 at their house 3 No 4 Yes

3 2 D 3 D 4 D 5 G 6 D

4 2 coming 3 is 4 coming 5 nice 6 can't 7 come 8 can

## Unit 10

1a 2 Salvador Dalí 3 Elvis Presley 4 Yo-Yo Ma 5 Indira Gandhi 6 Nelson Mandela 7 Luciano Pavarotti 8 Jane Austen 9 Eva Perón 10 Claude Monet

b 2 Argentinian 3 Italian 4 Colombian 5 South African 6 English 7 Spanish 8 French 9 Indian 10 Chinese

2 2 lived 3 went 4 worked 5 met 6 got married 7 became 8 became 9 died

3a 2 two thousand and one 3 nineteen twelve 4 eighteen forty-five 5 fourteen thirty-three

b 1 nineteen nineteen 2 nineteen thirty-four 3 nineteen forty-five 4 nineteen fifty-two

4a 2 worked 3 moved 4 studied 6 got 7 met 8 grew up 9 had

b 2 lived 3 went 4 studied 5 went 6 got 7 met 8 worked 9 got 10 had

5a 1 until 2 for 3 when 4 in 5 from; to

b 2 She studied at Kensington Business College 3 She was born 4 She worked at the Arab National Bank / She lived in Kuwait 5 She lived in Beirut / She went to school in Beirut

6 2 Where did you go to school?; e 3 What did you do after school?; d 4 What did you do in London?; c 5 How long did you stay in London?; a 6 What did you do after that?; f

7 2 water: b, c and d are food 3 beautiful: a, b and c are colours 4 woman: a, b and c are family 5 football: a, c and d are places to go 6 Russian: b, c and d are countries 7 slow: a, b and c are weather

8 1 Marta 2 Agi 3 Carlo 4 Nick

9 1N 2 – 3C, N, A, M 4M 5C, N 6C 7A 8 –

### 10 DVD-ROM Extra

2a 2 America 3 Stanford University 4 engineering 5 a restaurant 6 Palo Alto 7 five years 8 a company in Manchester 9 England

3 1 study 2 live in San Francisco 3 did you stay in America 4 were you there

4 1 Pakistan 2 America 3 to earn some money 4 California, near San Francisco 5 about 45 minutes from San Francisco

**b** **The adjectives in bold are wrong. Choose a different adjective.**

1 Go by bus. It's a ~~**noisy**~~ way to see London. *good*
2 They have a **fast** flat in London – just one room and a kitchen. ______
3 There are no cars in the street, so it's very **bad**. ______
4 Let's go by bus. Taxis are too **big**. ______
5 The food is **slow** here – only $1 for a large pizza. ______
6 She has a **cheap** car. She always drives at 130 kilometres an hour. ______

**GRAMMAR**
Present simple questions

**5 a** **Look at the questions. Add question words from the box.**

| What | When | Where |
|---|---|---|

**b** **Write the questions in the correct order. Then match them with answers a–f.**

1 When / get up / you / do / ?
*When do you get up?* [c]
2 on Saturday / you / do / What / do / ?
______ [ ]
3 you / How / to work / do / go / ?
______ [ ]
4 do / do / you / in the evening / What / ?
______ [ ]
5 Where / you / do / live / ?
______ [ ]
6 do / you / Where / have / lunch / ?
______ [ ]

a By bus.
b In a flat in Paris.
c At 6.30.
d Not much. I usually read then go to bed early.
e At work, usually. I just have a sandwich.
f I often go shopping.

**Over to you**

Choose three questions in 5b. Write answers.
*3 I usually go to work by bike.*

For more practice, go to Unit 6 of the Self-study DVD-ROM.

# EXPLORE Reading

6 a Read the travel information about Beijing.

You are in: Home » Practical Tips » **Getting around: Beijing Transport**

**Beijing Travel Advice**

- China Health and Travel Vaccination
- Beijing Travel Insurance
- Internet Access
- Chinese Visas
- Chinese Embassies Abroad
- Foreign Embassies in Beijing
- Chinese Telephones and Phone Cards
- Chinese Language Guide & Phrase Book
- Getting around: Beijing Transport
- Chinese Money & Currency Exchange
- « BACK TO MAIN

Beijing is big, but most tourists just go to a small area in the centre of the city.

**Beijing Transport: The Beijing Subway**

Click here for a Beijing subway map.

The Beijing subway is the best way to get around Beijing. There are seven main lines – five of them are new (built for the Beijing Olympics in 2008). The Beijing subway is very cheap, the service is good and it's very fast. There is just one problem – it's very crowded.

A single journey on the Beijing subway is 3 yuan – you can go anywhere.

**Beijing Transport: Taxis**

Beijing taxis are a really good way to get around and they're very cheap. They are about 10–20 yuan to go anywhere in the centre. Taxis are yellow and you can find them near bus stops.

Some taxi drivers speak English, but not all. Ask a Chinese friend or the hotel to write your address in Chinese, or show a business or hotel card.

**Beijing Transport: Buses**

Beijing buses are cheap, but they are slow and crowded and the roads are usually very busy. So, they're not a good way to get around Beijing.

**Beijing Transport: Bicycles**

Bicycle is a very good way to get round. It's quite slow, but you can see a lot. Many people in Beijing have cars now, but there are still lots of people on bikes.

Most hotels have bicycles for hire, and they're not expensive – they are about 10–50 yuan for one day.

b Choose words from the box and write them in the table.

cheap crowded fast slow

| Subway | Buses | Taxis | Bicycle |
|---|---|---|---|
| *cheap* | ______ | ______ | ______ |
| ______ | ______ | | ______ |
| ______ | ______ | | |
| ______ | | | |

7 Are these sentences true or false?

1 Beijing taxis are white. ☐
2 You can find taxis near a bus stop. ☐
3 All Beijing taxi drivers speak English. ☐
4 There are five subway lines. ☐
5 Lots of people cycle in Beijing. ☐
6 Buses are a good way to get around Beijing. ☐

8 Use a dictionary. Find the words in **bold**.

1 a small **area**
2 the **best** way
3 good **service**
4 a **single journey**
5 you can go **anywhere**
6 bicycles **for hire**

# DVD-ROM Extra How can I get to Haxby? 6

1 **Before you watch, think about your day. Write times.**

- I get up at ______ .
- I start work / school at ______ .
- I finish work / school at ______ .

2 **Watch the first part of the video. Yolanda talks about her day. Choose the correct words.**

On Thursday and Friday:
1 she gets up at 5 a.m. / 6 a.m.
2 she starts work at 5 a.m. / 6 a.m.
3 she works for 10 hours / 12 hours.
4 she has a Spanish class in the afternoon / evening.
5 she has dinner before / after her Spanish class.

3 **Yolanda talks about the evening. Tick the expressions you hear.**

come home ☑ have dinner ☐ watch TV ☐
go out with friends ☐ read a book ☐ go to bed ☐

4 **Watch the next part of the video. Answer the questions.**

1 Who lives in Haxby?
2 How can you get there?

5 **The station employee talks about two trains. Circle them in the timetable.**

| TRAINS | |
|---|---|
| **Manchester** | **York** |
| 16.28 | 17.58 |
| 17.28 | 18.58 |
| 18.04 | 20.04 |
| 19.04 | 21.15 |

6 **You want to go to Liverpool. Complete the conversation.**

| | |
|---|---|
| **YOU** | How can I [1]____________ to Liverpool, please? |
| **STATION EMPLOYEE** | Liverpool. You can [2]____________ there by train. The next train [3]____________ at 17.45. It [4]____________ in Liverpool at 18.20. It [5]____________ 35 minutes. |

| TRAINS | |
|---|---|
| **Manchester** | **Liverpool** |
| 17.45 | 18.20 |

# 7 Last week

GRAMMAR
Past simple

1 a Write the past forms of the verbs.

| Regular | | Irregular | |
|---|---|---|---|
| **Present** | **Past** | **Present** | **Past** |
| stay | 1 *stayed* | go | 4 *went* |
| listen | 2 ______ | have | 5 ______ |
| watch | 3 ______ | get | 6 ______ |
| | | meet | 7 ______ |

b Read what Margaret says. Add past verbs from 1a.

I had a nice quiet weekend. On Saturday, I 1______ breakfast in bed and 2______ to the radio. Then I 3______ up at about ten and I 4______ shopping. In the afternoon I 5______ my friend Elsie and we 6______ coffee together.
On Sunday, I 7______ for a walk by the river. Then in the evening, I 8______ at home and 9______ a film on television.

GRAMMAR
*was, were; wasn't, weren't*

2 a Read the emails. Add *was*, *were*, *wasn't* or *weren't*.

Sorry we 1 *weren't* at home last night. We 2______ out with friends. I'll call you tomorrow.

I 3______ ill last week, so I 4______ at work. But I'm OK now.

Sue and Paulo 5______ in the office on Monday – they 6______ both on holiday. They're back tomorrow.

I 7______ at Sonya's party on Saturday. It 8______ really good. Lots of my friends 9______ there.

b Write sentences from these notes. Use *was*, *were*, *wasn't* or *weren't*.

1 Sorry – I – not at home – at the cinema
*Sorry I wasn't at home. I was at the cinema.*
2 I – in London at the weekend – very interesting
______
3 Clara – not at the meeting on Monday – ill
______
4 We – in Barcelona last summer – the city – beautiful – our hotel – not very good
______
5 I – at Café Metro yesterday – very busy – lots of people there
______

**GRAMMAR** Questions with *was / were*

## 3 Complete the questions. Use words from the box.

| ~~were~~ were you like it was you |
|---|

**ROBERTO** Hi. 1 *Were* 2 ______ at the party last night?
**HASSAN** Yes, I was there.
**ROBERTO** What 3 ______ 4 ______ 5 ______?
**HASSAN** Oh, it wasn't very good. I went home early. Where 6 ______ 7 ______?
**ROBERTO** Oh, I stayed at home. I went to bed early.

**VOCABULARY** Place expressions

## 4 a Read about Seiko. Circle the correct preposition.

1 She was (at) / on work on Monday.
2 She was in / on holiday on Tuesday.
3 She was on / at a meeting on Tuesday morning.
4 She wasn't in / at home on Thursday evening.
5 She was in / at Tokyo on Friday.
6 She was on / at a party on Saturday.

**b** Look at Seiko's diary. Are sentences 1–6 true or false? Write T or F.

1 *F* 2 ☐ 3 ☐
4 ☐ 5 ☐ 6 ☐

**VOCABULARY**
Adjectives

**5** **Look at the information about books and hotels. Which is:**

1 a good book? [A]
2 a cheap book? [ ]
3 a long book? [ ]
4 a short book? [ ]
5 an expensive book? [ ]
6 a cheap hotel? [ ]
7 a big hotel? [ ]
8 a small hotel? [ ]
9 an expensive hotel? [ ]

**A** ***The Green Room***
by Anna Fulton

**Our price** ~~£15.95~~ £4.90
430 pages

3 reviews
"... a very interesting book."
"I loved this book."
"... the book of the year."

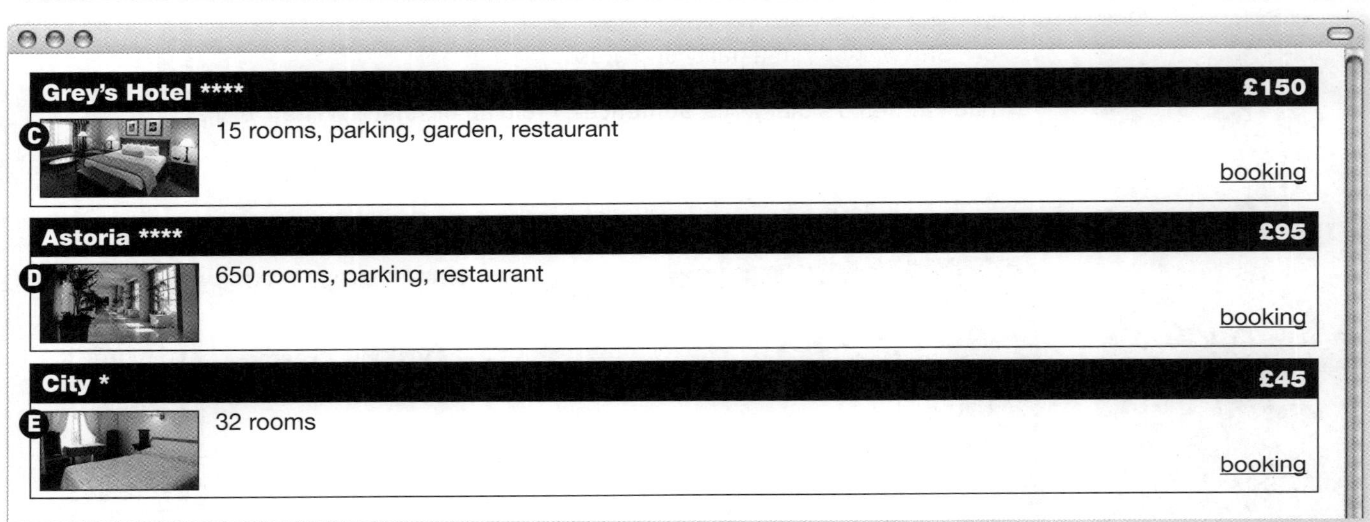


## TimeOut

**6** **Write words in the crossword.**

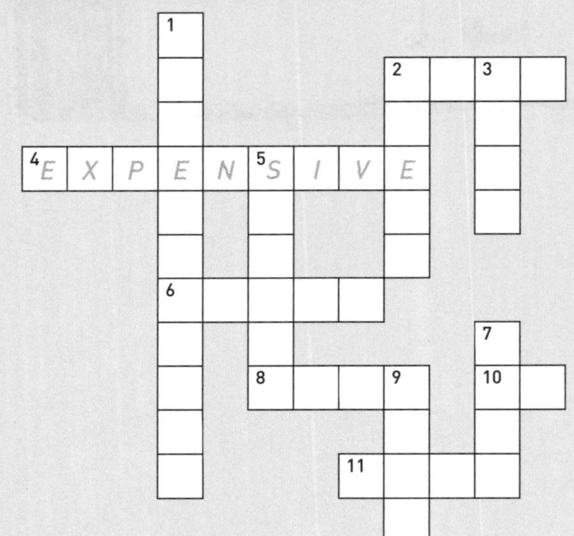


**Across (→)**

2 I want a drink. Let's go to a __________.
4 £150 for a bag! That's too __________.
6 It's a very __________ book, only 60 pages.
8 Not 6 across.
10 Maria isn't here. She's __________ holiday.
11 *The Green Room* is an interesting __________.

**Down (↓)**

1 *The Green Room* is an __________ book.
2 These jeans are __________. They're only €9.
3 You can see it at the cinema.
5 My son is 15. He's at __________.
7 No, I'm not at home. I'm still at __________.
9 Not bad!

# EXPLORE Writing

**7 a We can use *it* or *there* to join ideas.**

| | | |
|---|---|---|
| There's a new restaurant in our street. *The restaurant* opened last week. | → | There's a new restaurant in our street. **It** opened last week. (*it = the restaurant*) |
| There's a new restaurant in our street. We went *to the restaurant* last night. | → | There's a new restaurant in our street. We went **there** last night. (*there = to the restaurant*) |

**Change the words in bold to *it* or *there*.**

1. I saw a film last night. I didn't like **the film**. ___*it*___
2. Can you come to the meeting? **The meeting** is at 3 o'clock. ________
3. Kim was at the party. I saw him **at the party**. ________
4. I love Italy. I went **to Italy** on holiday last year. ________
5. I went to Hamburg last week. We have friends **in Hamburg**. ________

**b Look at paragraphs A and B. Then answer the questions.**

1. How many sentences are in paragraph A? ______
2. How many sentences are in paragraph B? ______
3. What words are in B, but not in A? ______, ______, ______, ______, ______

**A** "I had a free day on Tuesday. I went into town. I went shopping. Then I met a friend. There's a new restaurant in town. We had lunch in the restaurant. We had a nice time. The food wasn't very good. The food was very expensive."

**B** "I had a free day on Tuesday, so I went into town and went shopping. Then I met a friend. There's a new restaurant in town, so we had lunch there together. We had a nice time, but the food wasn't very good and it was very expensive."

**c Join these sentences. Use *and*, *so* or *but* and *it* or *there*.**

1. There was a new James Bond film. We went to see the James Bond film.
   *There was a new James Bond film, so we* ____________________
2. *Titanic* is a very good film. *Titanic* is very long.
   ____________________
3. I went to the café at six. My friends weren't at the café.
   ____________________
4. In 2005, I lived in London. I met my husband in London.
   ____________________

**Writing reference and practice, p56**

# DVD-ROM Extra Last weekend

1 **Before you watch, think about last weekend. Which sentences are true for you?**

- I stayed at home.
- I visited someone.
- I went to the cinema.
- I met friends.
- I listened to music.
- I went to a restaurant.

2 **Watch the video. Who did these things? Write Y (= Yolanda), W (= Wai Kee) or both.**

1 listened to music ___W___
2 visited a friend ______
3 stayed at home ______
4 went to see a film ______
5 met friends ______
6 went to a restaurant ______

3 **Watch Yolanda again. Match the adjectives with 1–4.**

~~good~~ terrible long boring wonderful expensive

1 her weekend ___good___
2 the restaurant __________
3 the food __________
4 the film __________, __________, __________

4 **Watch Wai Kee again. Circle the correct answers.**

| On Saturday, he | went out<br>stayed at home | and | watched a film.<br>went to the cinema. |
|---|---|---|---|

| Yesterday, he | stayed at home<br>met friends | and | had lunch<br>had dinner | at home.<br>in a restaurant. |
|---|---|---|---|---|

5 **Are these sentences true (T) or false (F) ? Watch the video again to check.**

1 Yolanda visited a friend in York. ☐
2 They went to a Chinese restaurant called Lee Garden. ☐
3 The film was called *No Country for Young Men*. ☐
4 Wai Kee doesn't know York. ☐

6 **You are Yolanda. Answer Wai Kee's questions.**

**WAI KEE** Good weekend?
**YOLANDA** ______________________________
**WAI KEE** Were you at home?
**YOLANDA** ______________________________
**WAI KEE** Where were you?
**YOLANDA** ______________________________

# 8 Places

**GRAMMAR**
Past simple positive and negative

1 a **Add verbs to the table.**

| ⊕ | ⊖ |
|---|---|
| I went | I [1] *didn't go* |
| I saw | I [2] ________ |
| I [3] ________ | I didn't buy |
| I ate | I [5] ________ |
| I [5] ________ | I didn't stay |
| I visited | I [6] ________ |
| I [7] ________ | I didn't have |

b **Read about London and then read Marco's email.**

See Buckingham Palace

Go on a London bus

Have lunch in a pub

Visit the British Museum

See St Paul's Cathedral

Go shopping at Camden Market

Go to London Zoo

Marco

I only had one afternoon in London, so I didn't see much. I saw Buckingham Palace and I had lunch in a pub. Then I went by taxi to the airport.

c **Complete the sentences. Use verbs from the table in 1a.**

1 Marco ________ Buckingham Palace.
2 He ________ St Paul's Cathedral.
3 He ________ shopping.
4 He ________ lunch in a pub.
5 He ________ to London Zoo.
6 He ________ the British Museum.

**VOCABULARY** Expressions with *go*

**2** **Look at the photos. Complete the emails. Use words from the box.**

sightseeing restaurants camping swimming skiing shopping

We had a great holiday. We went [1]__________ every day and in the evening we went to [2]__________ .

We had a nice time. We went [3]__________ near the sea and we went [4]__________ every day.

We stayed in London for two days and we went [5]__________ .

We saw Buckingham Palace and St Paul's Cathedral.

And we went [6]__________ and bought lots of clothes.

**GRAMMAR** Past simple questions

**3** **Read the conversation. Make questions from the notes.**

**EVA** [1] you – have a good time – New York?
**ANNA** Yes, it was really good.
**EVA** [2] you – stay – hotel?
**ANNA** No, I stayed with friends.
**EVA** [3] you – go – sightseeing?
**ANNA** Yes. I saw a lot and I took lots of photos.
**EVA** [4] you – go – Central Park?
**ANNA** Yes, we went there one afternoon. It was really nice.

1 *Did you have a good time in New York?*
2 ____________________
3 ____________________
4 ____________________

**VOCABULARY**
Months

4 a **Write the months in the puzzle.**

1 April, _________, June
2 _________, November, December
3 _________, July, August
4 August, _________, October
5 February, _________, April
6 June, July, _________
7 These words are all _________ of the year.

7↓
1 M A Y
2
3
4
5
6

b **Write the months correctly.**

1 His birthday is in **rynuaJa**. *January*
2 School starts in **reStbemep**. ___________
3 I was in England last **liprA**. ___________
4 They're on holiday in **ubraFeyr**. ___________
5 It's usually cold here in **reNvomeb** and **meDerceb**. ___________ , ___________

**Writing reference and practice, Capitals (2) p55**

**VOCABULARY**
Weather, seasons

5 **Find pairs of words. Write them in the list. Which word is not in a pair?**

coolwetsummerhotdrywintersunnycoldwarm

*cool* – *warm*
_________ – _________
_________ – _________
_________ – _________

_________

**GRAMMAR**
*Wh-* questions

6 **Put the words in order. Then match them with the answers.**

1 you / did / stay / Where / ?
*Where did you stay?* [c]
2 did / do / you / What / in New York / ?
_________________________ [ ]
3 the weather / was / What / like ?
_________________________ [ ]
4 go / there / When / you / did / ?
_________________________ [ ]
5 you / did / How / go / there / ?
_________________________ [ ]
6 with / did / you / Who / go / ?
_________________________ [ ]

a Last month.
b By plane from London.
c In a hotel in Manhattan.
d Not very nice. It was very cold.
e With two people from work.
f It was a business trip, so I went to lots of meetings.

# EXPLORE Reading

7 Read about hotels in Munich, Germany. Then read the reviews. Which hotel are they about? Write A, B or C.

1 ______ 2 ______ 3 ______

A

## Mimosa Hotel

**Room price: €65** Check rates

A small hotel near the centre of Munich, you can walk to the city centre from here. Near an underground station, so you can easily get to other parts of the city. The rooms are small and comfortable, with TV, telephone, mini bar and bathroom.

read reviews write a review

B

## Plaza Palace Hotel

**Room price: €135** Check rates

The Plaza Palace Hotel is next to Munich International Airport, so you can walk to Terminals 1 and 2. The hotel has 343 modern, comfortable rooms, all with desk, mini bar, telephone, cable and pay TV and high-speed Internet. Two restaurants and a large bar area. Swimming pool, sauna.

read reviews write a review

C

## Europa Inn

**Room price: €73** Check rates

The Europa Inn is about five minutes by underground from the city centre. The hotel is in Schwabing, the university area of the city, and there are cafés, restaurants and shops near the hotel. There are 362 air-conditioned rooms, with high-speed Internet and W-Lan. Guests can use the new Business Centre, the indoor swimming pool and sauna.

read reviews write a review

1 **Review**

**Great for a business trip!!** By Scott B

I always stay here when I'm in Munich on business. The place is so clean! Great service, big modern rooms and (very important!) the best breakfast buffet in Germany. And just a short walk to the check-in at the airport. It is expensive, but you don't need to get a taxi to the airport.

2 **Review**

**One night in Munich** By Irwco

The hotel was clean and the bed was comfortable. It is close to the university and the English garden. There is breakfast in the hotel restaurant but it is €20!! The cost of parking and breakfast for me and my son was 40% of my bill!!

3 **Review**

**Lovely!** By finng

I stayed there last month – a really lovely hotel, not too expensive. The rooms are small but very comfortable and the public area – bar and restaurant – was beautiful and a great place to sit. There is good shopping near the hotel, but the hotel is on a quiet street.

8 **Choose the hotel. Write A, B or C.**

1 It's near the airport. ______
2 It's in the city centre. ______
3 It's good for business people. ______
4 The rooms are expensive. ______
5 It has small rooms. ______
6 It has a swimming pool. ______, ______
7 It's near the shops. ______

9 **Use a dictionary. Find the words in bold.**

1 You can **easily** get to other parts of the city.
2 The rooms are **comfortable**.
3 The place is so **clean**!
4 40% of my **bill**

1 A friend says "I went to Egypt last week." Before you watch, think of questions to ask him / her.

- Did you ...?
- Where ...?
- What ...?
- Who ...?
- How long ...?

2 Watch the video. Complete the sentences. Use expressions from the box.

| ~~on holiday~~ a great time his brother do much relaxed to Cairo five days |
|---|

1 Duggal was *on holiday* last week.
2 He went ____________.
3 He stayed with ____________.
4 He stayed for ____________.
5 He had ____________.
6 They didn't ____________.
7 They just ____________.

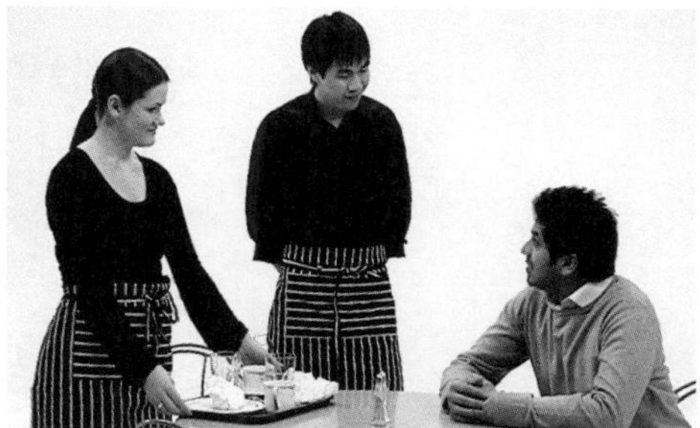

3 Wai Kee and Yolanda ask questions. Match the two parts of the questions.

1 Where did you
2 Did you
3 How long did you
4 What was it
5 What did you

a stay in a hostel or a hotel?
b stay?
c do?
d like?
e go?

4 Duggal talks about these things. What does he say about them?

1 sightseeing ____________________
2 his brother ____________________
3 the food ____________________
4 people from Cairo ____________________

5 Watch again. You are Duggal. Ask Wai Kee questions.

**WAI KEE** I went to Cairo last year.
**DUGGAL** 1 *When* ____________________?
**WAI KEE** In January.
**DUGGAL** 2 ____________________?
**WAI KEE** With my friend Jae.
**DUGGAL** 3 ____________________?
**WAI KEE** In a hostel near the market.

# 9 Going out

**VOCABULARY**
Telephone expressions

**1 a Write the sentences and questions in the correct order.**

1 busy / I'm / now / just *I'm busy just now.*
2 I / call / you / later / Can / ? ______
3 you / busy / Are / ? ______
4 later / call / I'll / you ______

**b Write the conversation.**

> "Hi Igor it's Hanna oh hi Hanna how are you I'm fine are you busy yes I'm still at work is it important no never mind I'll call you this evening yes call me at about 8.00 OK bye"

HANNA 1 *Hi, Igor. It's Hanna.*
IGOR 2 ______
HANNA 3 ______
IGOR 4 ______
HANNA 5 ______
IGOR 6 ______
HANNA 7 ______

**GRAMMAR**
Present progressive

**2 a Write the *-ing* forms.**

1 watch *watching*
2 have ______
3 listen ______
4 cook ______
5 go ______
6 write ______
7 eat ______
8 talk ______

**b What are they doing? Write sentences with verbs from 2a. Begin *He's …* , *She's …* , *They're …* .**

1 
2 
3 

4 
5 
6 
7 
8 

1 *He's having a shower.*
2 ______
3 ______
4 ______
5 ______
6 ______
7 ______
8 ______

**GRAMMAR**
Present progressive – questions

**3** **Read the phone conversations. The sentences in bold are wrong. Write them correctly.**

A Hello, Tom. Are you OK?
B [1]**Yes, I fine.**
A [2]**You watching TV?**
B [3]**No, I read a book.**

1 *Yes, I'm fine.*
2 ______________________
3 ______________________

A Hi Ahmed. [4]**What you are doing?**
B [5]**I just having lunch.** How about you?
A I'm on the bus. [6]**I just go to work.**

4 ______________________
5 ______________________
6 ______________________

**VOCABULARY**
Future time expressions

**4** **Read what Alija says. Today is Tuesday, 11 June. Complete her diary.**

1 "Next Tuesday, I'm going to the hairdresser."
2 "I'm not going out tonight. I'm too tired, and there's a good film on TV at 8.15."
3 "I'm going to a party next Wednesday."
4 "I'm visiting my parents this weekend."
5 "I'm getting up early tomorrow morning. There's an office meeting at 9.00."
6 "Let's meet for coffee tomorrow. How about 4.30?"
7 "We're going to the cinema on Thursday. Would you like to come?"

**Over to you**
Think of three things you are doing this week or next week. Write sentences like in 4.

# TimeOut

5 Write words in the crossword.

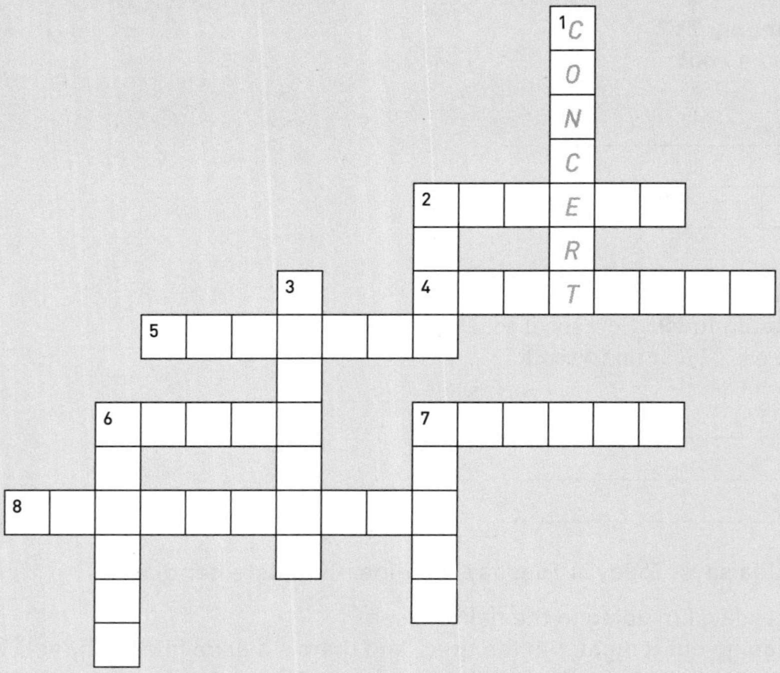


**Across (→)**

2 Go there to see a film.

4 Do you want to come to the ___________ match on Saturday?

5 Go there to see a play by Shakespeare.

6 We stayed at the Plaza Palace ___________.

7 Go there to see old things.

8 Go there to have a meal.

**Down (↓)**

1 Go there to listen to music.

2 Go there to have coffee or a drink.

3 Go to an art ___________ to look at paintings.

6 The Lighthouse is a ___________ in Rio de Janeiro.

7 Do you want to come to the football ___________ on Saturday?

# EXPLORE Writing

**6 a** **Look at these sentences about Cairo.**

> We only had one day in Cairo and this was it! So we got up early and went to the souk, which is an area of streets with shops and markets.

**Notice how we use *which* to join ideas:**

| | | |
|---|---|---|
| We went to the souk.<br>The souk is an area of streets with shops and markets. | → | 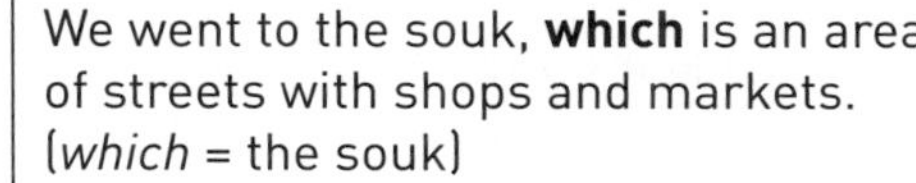 We went to the souk, **which** is an area of streets with shops and markets.<br>(*which* = the souk) |

**To talk about people, we use *who*:**

| | | |
|---|---|---|
| We talked to the hotel manager.<br>He told us how to get to the souk. | → | 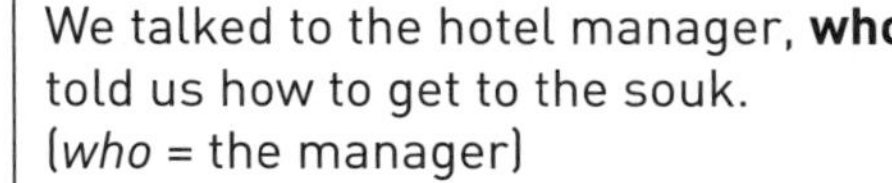 We talked to the hotel manager, **who** told us how to get to the souk.<br>(*who* = the manager) |

**Write *who* or *which* in the gaps.**

1 We sat by the River Nile in the evening, ______ was very beautiful.
2 We stayed at the Windsor Hotel, ______ was clean and not too expensive.
3 We talked to some Egyptian students, ______ were at Cairo University.
4 Anna bought a coffee pot, ______ was about $15.
5 In the evening we met a friend from the USA, ______ lives in Cairo with his family.

**b** **Look at paragraphs A and B.**

1 What words are in paragraph B, but not in A?
2 How many sentences are in paragraph A, and how many are in paragraph B?

**A**

> The next day we flew to Mumbai, in India. We stayed with an old friend. Our friend lives in Mumbai. Our friend works in a bank. We spent three days in Mumbai. Mumbai is a very big, noisy city. Mumbai has a good atmosphere.

**B**

> The next day we flew to Mumbai, in India and stayed with an old friend, who lives there and works in a bank. We spent three days in Mumbai, which is a very big, noisy city, but it has a good atmosphere.

**c** **Write this paragraph again, so it has only two sentences. Use words from the box.**

| so | who | there | and | which |
|---|---|---|---|---|

> Last year I went to Madrid. I stayed with a friend. My friend teaches English in Madrid. She lives next to a restaurant. The restaurant has very good fish and meat dishes. We ate in the restaurant every evening.

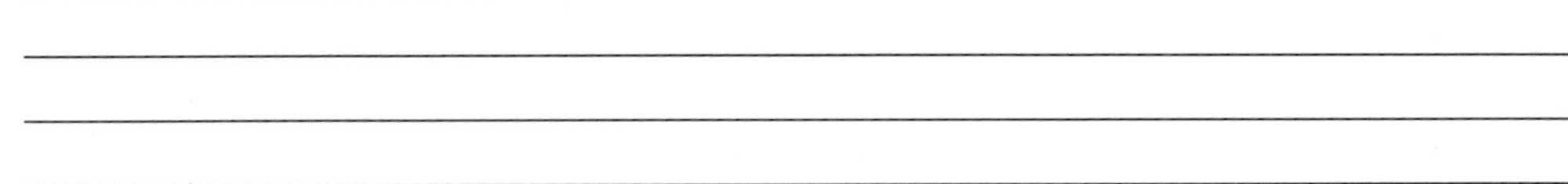

*Last year I went to Madrid and* ______________________________

______________________________

______________________________

______________________________

**Writing reference and practice, *who, which, where,* p57**

For more practice, go to Unit 9 of the Self-study DVD-ROM. 

# DVD-ROM Extra Are you busy?

**1 Before you watch, look at the photo of Duggal.**

- Where is he?
- What is he doing?

**2 Watch the video and answer the questions.**

1 Who is having a party? ______
2 Where is it? When is it? ______
3 Can Duggal come? ______
4 Is Paula free on Sunday? ______

**3 Watch Duggal and Giacomo again. Who says these things? Write D(uggal) or G(iacomo).**

1 What are you doing? _G_
2 I'm busy just now. ______
3 I'm talking to Paula. ______
4 Can I call you later? ______
5 OK, fine. ______
6 Bye. ______

**4 Watch Duggal and Paula again. What do they say?**

**DUGGAL** A friend from London [1] _is_ [2] ______ to stay with me on Saturday.
**DUGGAL** Giacomo [3] ______ [4] ______ to my house for dinner.
**PAULA** That sounds [5] ______.
**PAULA** Simon [6] ______ [7] ______. He's busy, but I [8] ______.

**5 You invite Duggal to a party. Complete the conversation.**

**YOU** I'm having _a party_. ______?
**DUGGAL** Yes, I'd love to come. What day?
**YOU** ______.
**DUGGAL** OK. What time?
**YOU** ______.
**DUGGAL** OK, thank you. I'll see you there.

# 10 People's lives

**VOCABULARY** Nationalities, jobs

**1 a Look in the box. Find:**

1 a Colombian writer. *Gabriel García Márquez*
2 a Spanish painter. ______
3 an American singer. ______
4 a Chinese musician. ______
5 an Indian leader. ______
6 a South African leader. ______
7 an Italian singer. ______
8 an English writer. ______
9 an Argentinian leader. ______
10 a French painter. ______

If you don't know the answers, look at www.wikipedia.org!

~~Gabriel García Márquez~~ Indira Gandhi Eva Perón Elvis Presley Nelson Mandela Yo-Yo Ma Luciano Pavarotti Claude Monet Salvador Dalí Jane Austen

**b Add the words from 1a.**

| Country | Nationality |
|---|---|
| USA | 1 *American* |
| Argentina | 2 ______ |
| Italy | 3 ______ |
| Colombia | 4 ______ |
| South Africa | 5 ______ |
| England | 6 ______ |
| Spain | 7 ______ |
| France | 8 ______ |
| India | 9 ______ |
| China | 10 ______ |

**VOCABULARY** Past simple verbs

**2 Read about Eva Perón. Add verbs from the box.**

~~was born~~ died became (x 2) met lived worked got married went

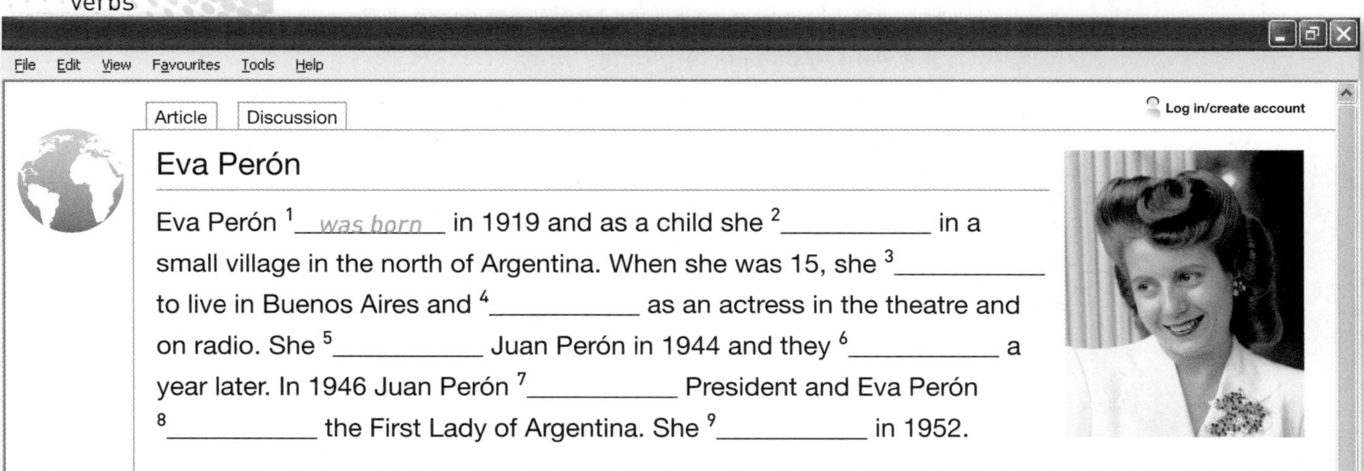


## Eva Perón

Eva Perón [1] *was born* in 1919 and as a child she [2] ______ in a small village in the north of Argentina. When she was 15, she [3] ______ to live in Buenos Aires and [4] ______ as an actress in the theatre and on radio. She [5] ______ Juan Perón in 1944 and they [6] ______ a year later. In 1946 Juan Perón [7] ______ President and Eva Perón [8] ______ the First Lady of Argentina. She [9] ______ in 1952.

**VOCABULARY** Years

**3 a Write the years. Use words from the box.**

nineteen ~~sixty~~ and thousand fourteen three eighteen ~~four~~ two twelve thirty ~~seventeen~~ forty one five

1 1764 *seventeen sixty-four*
2 2001 ______
3 1912 ______
4 1845 ______
5 1433 ______

**b Complete these sentences. Write the years as words.**

1 Eva Perón was born in ______.
2 She went to Buenos Aires in ______.
3 She married Juan Perón in ______.
4 She died in ______.

**VOCABULARY** Life events

**4 a Write the past forms of the verbs.**

| Regular | | Irregular | |
|---|---|---|---|
| live | 1 *lived* | go | 5 *went* |
| work | 2 ______ | get | 6 ______ |
| move | 3 ______ | meet | 7 ______ |
| study | 4 ______ | grow up | 8 ______ |
| | | have | 9 ______ |

**b Write what Sheena says. Add past verbs from 4a.**

I [1] *grew up* in Scotland – my family [2] ______ in a small town near Glasgow. And I [3] ______ to university in Glasgow – I [4] ______ medicine. Then after university I [5] ______ to live in Canada, in Toronto – I [6] ______ a job in a hospital there. I [7] ______ my husband in Toronto, that was in 2003, when I was 24. He [8] ______ in the same hospital – he's a doctor. And we [9] ______ married a year later. And then in 2005, I [10] ______ a baby – a boy called Alan. And we live just near Toronto.

**GRAMMAR** Past time expressions

**5 a Read these sentences about Sheena. Choose the best word.**

1 She lived in Scotland for / until / when she was 22.
2 She was at university in / for / until four years.
3 She went to Canada for / until / when she was 22.
4 She went to Canada for / in / until 2001.
5 She lived in Scotland from / until / to 1982 from / to / when 2001.

**b** Look at Zeinab's life. Complete the sentences.

Zeinab Hamzawi
born 16.02.1984
1997 – 2005
Beirut International School, Beirut, Lebanon
2005 – 2007
Kensington Business College, London
2007 – 2010
Arab National Bank, Kuwait

1 *She went to Beirut International School* when she was 13.
2 ______ for two years.
3 ______ in 1984.
4 ______ from 2007 to 2010.
5 ______ until 2005.

GRAMMAR
Questions

**6** Someone asks Zeinab questions. Write them and match with the answers.

1 you / When / were / born / ?
*When were you born?* [B]
2 did / you / to school / Where / go / ?
______ [ ]
3 after school / you / did / do / What / ?
______ [ ]
4 did / you / do / What / in London?
______ [ ]
5 in London / stay / you / did / How long / ?
______ [ ]
6 What / after that / did / do / you / ?
______ [ ]

a For two years, from 2005 to 2007
b In 1984.
c I went to a business college.
d I went to London for two years
e In Beirut, in Lebanon
f I got a job with a bank in Kuwait.

**Over to you**

Write four questions like 1 – 6 which you can answer.
*What did you do after school?*
Then write answers to the questions.
*I went to university.*

**Writing reference and practice, *when, before, after,* p57**

# TimeOut

**7** One word is different from the others. Underline it and say why.

1 a waiter b cleaner c computer d salesman *a, b and d are jobs*
2 a water b meat c vegetables d rice ______
3 a red b green c grey d beautiful ______
4 a daughter b brother c father d woman ______
5 a art gallery b football c theatre d cinema ______
6 a Russian b Germany c Japan d Brazil ______
7 a wet b cold c slow d sunny ______

# EXPLORE Reading

ad = advertisement

**8** **These people all want a job. Read the ads. Which person:**

1 wants to work in a family? ____________
2 can work in an office or hotel? ____________
3 is a waiter? ____________
4 wants to work in a shop? ____________

**Homepage > Jobs > Work Wanted**

## Looking for a job ...

**Date posted:** Tue 21 April **Save** **Share** **Print**

I'm from Italy, but I live in London and I'm looking for a job in a restaurant or café. I worked in a café for six months, then in a Spanish tapas bar. I speak good English, I'm hard-working and I like to work with people.
Contact Carlo 0772-6543792.

**Click here to reply**

**Date posted:** Wed 22 April **Save** **Share** **Print**

I'm Nick Swan. I'm 17, I live in east London. I left school six months ago and I'm looking for work in a shop or a supermarket. I can work in the day or in the evening. I'm honest and hard-working. Please phone me on 0771-624630.

**Click here to reply**

**Date posted:** Wed 22 April **Save** **Share** **Print**

Hi. My name is Agi, from Poland. I'm a professional cleaner, very good at my job. I cleaned offices for one year in Poland and now I'm living in London. My rate is £8–10 an hour. I speak some English. Please send me an email agi88@wp.pl or text me: 07835691.

**Click here to reply**

**Date posted:** Wed 22 April **Save** **Share** **Print**

I'm Marta. I'm a Mexican student. I came to London last year to learn English and worked with a family for six months. Now I'm looking for a new job. I can cook, help in the house and look after children. I speak good English. Please contact me by email: mj30@wp.net.

**Click here to reply**

**9** **Choose the person (or people). Write C, N, A , M or – .**

1 He / she is English. ______
2 He / she doesn't speak English. ______
3 He / she lives in London. ______
4 He / she is a student. ______
5 You can phone him / her. ______
6 He / she worked in a café. ______
7 He / she worked in an office. ______
8 He / she worked in a shop. ______

**10** **Can you guess the words in bold? Use a dictionary to check.**

1 **I'm looking for** a job
2 I left school **six months ago**.
3 I'm **honest** and **hard-working**.
4 My **rate** is £8–10
5 I can **help** in the house.
6 I can **look after** children.

**1** **Before you watch, look at the photo.**

- Who are the people?
- What are they doing?
- What do you think they are saying?

**2 a** **In the video, Duggal talks about his past life. What do you think he says? Before you watch, complete the sentences with words from the box.**

| ~~Pakistan~~ | America | England |
|---|---|---|
| five years | Stanford University | |
| a restaurant | a company in Manchester | |
| engineering | Palo Alto | |

1 I grew up in *Pakistan* ____________.
2 I went to university in ____________.
3 I studied at ____________.
4 I studied ____________.
5 I worked in ____________.
6 I lived in ____________.
7 I stayed for ____________.
8 I got a job with ____________.
9 I moved to ____________.

**b** **Watch the video to check.**

**3** **Paula and Giacomo ask questions. What are they?**

**PAULA** Where [1] *did you* ____________?
**DUGGAL** At Stanford.

**GIACOMO** Did you [2] ____________?
**DUGGAL** No, Palo Alto.

**PAULA** How long [3] ____________?
**DUGGAL** Five years.

**PAULA** When [4] ____________?
**DUGGAL** From 1995 to 2000

**4** **Answer the questions.**

1 Where did Duggal go to school?
____________
2 Where did he learn to cook?
____________
3 Why did he work in a restaurant?
____________
4 Where is Stanford?
____________
5 Where is Palo Alto?
____________

# Writing reference and practice

## Punctuation

| | |
|---|---|
| . | full stop |
| , | comma |
| ? | question mark |
| ! | exclamation mark |
| ' | apostrophe |

Use **.** (= full stop) at the end of a sentence:

*Hi, I'm Alma.*
*This is my husband.*

Use **,** (= comma) to show a pause in the middle of a sentence:

*Hi, I'm Alma, and this is my husband, Yussef.*
*I bought a jacket, trousers, a shirt and a tie.*
*We went for a walk, and then we went to a café for lunch.*

Use **?** (= question mark) at the end of a question:

*What's your name?*
*Are you married?*

Use **!** (= exclamation mark) in expressions like:

*Happy birthday!*
*Oh, sorry!*
*Hi!*

Use **'** (= apostrophe) to show a letter (or letters) is not there:

*He's still at work* (= *He* ***is***)
*Where's the kitchen?* (= *Where* ***is***)
*I'm having breakfast.* (= *I* ***am***)
*I can't come to the party.* (= *can* ***no****t*)

### PRACTICE

**These sentences and questions are from the Coursebook. Add punctuation. Then look in the Coursebook to check.**

1 Im Mike

*I'm Mike.* ______ (p6)

2 Whats your name

______ (p6)

3 Hi Jo Im your new teacher

______ (p6)

4 Wheres London

______ (p8)

5 Its in England

______ (p8)

6 I have three children two boys and a girl

______ (p10)

7 Hi how are you

______ (p12)

8 We have a big kitchen where we eat

______ (p12)

# Capital letters (1)

| Small letters | Capital (= big) letters |
|---|---|
| a, b, c, d ... | A, B, C, D ... |

Use a capital letter for:

**the word 'I':**
***I*** *work in an office.*
*Can* ***I*** *have a sandwich?*

**the start of a sentence:**
***T****his is my daughter.*
***S****he's 22.*

**names of people:**
*My name is* ***M****ary* ***G****reen.*

**names of towns:**
*I'm from* ***S****ingapore.*

**countries, nationalities and languages:**
*She's from* ***M****exico.*
*She's* ***M****exican.*
*She speaks* ***S****panish.*

## PRACTICE

**These sentences are from the Coursebook. Add punctuation and capital letters. Then look in the Coursebook to check.**

1 hello im mary green
*Hello, I'm Mary Green.* ____ (p6)

2 are you from the usa
____ (p7)

3 im from london
____ (p7)

4 i have a room in a big flat in berlin with six other students this is normal in germany we have a big kitchen where we eat
____
____
____ (p12)

# Capital letters (2)

Use a capital letter for:

**names of films and books:**
*My favourite book is* ***T****he* ***A****lchemist by Paulo Coehlo.*

**names of cars, companies ...:**
*My car is a* ***T****oyota.*
*He works for* ***M****icrosoft.*

**days and months:**
*on* ***T****uesday*
*next* ***F****riday*
*in* ***S****eptember*
*last* ***M****ay*

## PRACTICE

**These paragraphs are from the Coursebook. Add punctuation and capital letters. Then look in the Coursebook to check.**

1 the train leaves moscow every day it goes through siberia to irkutsk then through mongolia to china the journey is about 9,000 kilometres and it takes six days you can sleep eat and drink tea on the train and people also sell food at the stations
*The train leaves Moscow* ____
____
____
____
____
____
____ (p52)

2 cancun mexico
cancun is always hot its dry and sunny from december to july from august to november its hot and very wet
____
____
____
____ (p66)

3 lighthouse hostel rio do janeiro brazil
this is a small quiet hostel in ipanema its only a few minutes from the beach and there are restaurants shops bars and clubs near the hostel we have one lovely room for two to four people and a dormitory with eight beds
____
____
____
____
____
____
____ (p96)

## he, she, it, they, there

Use *he, she, it, they, there* so you don't use the same noun again:

*I live in Naples.* ***It****'s a town in Florida.* (*it* = Naples).
*I eat lots of bananas.* ***They****'re very cheap.* (*they* = bananas)
*My husband isn't at home.* ***He****'s still at work.* (*he* = my husband)
*I work for Rolls-Royce in Bristol. They have a large office* ***there****.* (*there* = in Bristol)
*We like Italy. We often go* ***there*** *on holiday.* (*there* = to Italy)

### PRACTICE

**These sentences are from the Coursebook. Change the words in bold. Use *he, she, it* or *there*. Then check in the Coursebook.**

1 My parents live in Halifax. **My parents** have a house **in Halifax**. (p18)

*My parents live in Halifax. They have* ______________________

______________________

2 My brother lives in Australia. **My brother** has an Australian wife and three children. (p18)

______________________

______________________

3 Dino's is a small Italian café. **Dino's** is expensive, but they have good ice cream and very good coffee. **Dino's** is in Green Street, near the station. (p23)

______________________

______________________

______________________

4 People drink tea in cups. **People** make **tea** quite strong and drink **tea** with milk and sometimes sugar.

______________________

______________________ (p36)

## and, but, or, so, because

Use *and, but, or* to join sentences:

*I met a friend. We went shopping together.*
→ *I met a friend* ***and*** *we went shopping together.*

*I went to IKEA on Saturday. I didn't buy anything.*
→ *I went to IKEA on Saturday,* ***but*** *I didn't buy anything.*

*Do you want to go out? Shall we stay at home?*
→ *Do you want to go out,* ***or*** *shall we stay at home?*

Use *so* and *because* to say why.

*The flat is quite noisy. It's in the town centre.*
→ *The flat is quite noisy* ***because*** *it's in the town centre.*
→ *The flat is in the town centre,* ***so*** *it's quite noisy.*

### PRACTICE

**1 These sentences are from the Coursebook. Add *and, but* or *or* in the gaps. Then look in the Coursebook to check.**

1 We're married *but* we have no children. (p10)
2 I have two brothers _______ no sisters. We're a big family – most people have two children, _______ maybe just one child. (p20)
3 Dino's is a small Italian café. It's expensive, _______ they have good ice cream _______ very good coffee. (p23)
4 Friday is a holiday _______ many people go to the mosque, _______ most shops are open. (p28)
5 In most offices, men wear a suit _______ a tie, _______ a jacket _______ trousers. (p44)

**2 Add *and, but, so* or *because* in the gaps. Then look in the Coursebook to check.**

1 Sunday is a holiday, *and* many people go to church, _____________ some shops are open. (p28)
2 Many people drink green tea. People make it in a small teapot, _____________ drink it in small cups. It's quite weak, _____________ you can drink two or three cups of it. (p36)
3 The river is very wide, _____________ you don't see a lot. Bring a hammock to sleep in _____________ lots of books to read! (p52)
4 My mother helped her _____________ she was a girl, _____________ the men in the family didn't help at all. (p60)
5 My husband works at home, _____________ he usually cooks the meals. (p60)

## who, which, where

Use *who, which, where* to say more about people, things and places:

*We stayed with my brother. He lives in Dubai.*
→ *We stayed with my brother,* ***who*** *lives in Dubai.*

*I went to the Museum of Modern Art. It's in the centre of Manhattan.*
→ *I went to the Museum of Modern Art,* ***which*** *is in the centre of Manhattan.*

*Picasso moved to Paris. He met Henri Matisse there.*
→ *Picasso moved to Paris,* ***where*** *he met Henri Matisse.*

### PRACTICE

**These sentences are from the Coursebook. Add *who, which* or *where* in the gaps. Then look in the Coursebook.**

1 We got up early and went to the souk, ____________ is an area of streets with shops and markets. (p62)

2 In Germany, the person ____________ has the birthday often invites friends and family for a meal in a restaurant and he or she pays for it. (p92)

3 The hostel has a big living room ____________ you can talk to people, watch TV or listen to music. (p93)

## when, before, after

Use *when, before, after* to say when things happened:

*I was in the USA. I worked in a restaurant.*
→ ***When*** *I was in the USA, I worked in a restaurant.*

*I left university. I got a job in Tokyo.*
→ ***After*** *I left university, I got a job in Tokyo.*

*I had Spanish lessons. I went to Argentina.*
→ *I had Spanish lessons* ***before*** *I went to Argentina.*

### PRACTICE

**These sentences are from the Coursebook. Add *when, before* or *after* in the gaps. Then look in the Coursebook to check.**

1 Some people have a cup of tea in bed in the morning ____________ they start the day. (p36)

2 ____________ my mother was a child, only women did housework. (p60)

3 ____________ they got married, they lived together in Mexico City, in a house in Coyoacan, which is now a museum. (p84)

4 ____________ a child has a birthday, parents put all the presents by the bed in the night, so the child will find them ____________ he or she wakes up. (p92)

5 ____________ he was seven, his father died and he went to live with his grandmother. (p92)

6 The painter Pablo Picasso was born in 1881 in Malaga, Spain. ____________ he was 13, his family moved to Barcelona. (p94)

# Acknowledgements

**Adrian Doff** would like to thank Karen Momber and Keith Sands at Cambridge University Press for overseeing the project and for their invaluable help and support throughout the development of this course. He would also like to thank his editor, Andrew Reid, for his commitment and hard work and his help in bringing the book into its final form.

He would like to thank Dr Astrid Krake and Donna Liersch at the Volkshochschule München for giving him an opportunity to teach there and try out new ideas.

He would also like to thank Gabriella Zaharias for consistently supporting and encouraging him during the writing of this book.

**Nick Robinson** would also like to thank Anna Barnard.

Text design and page make-up: Stephanie White at Kamae Design
Picture research: Hilary Luckcock

**The publishers are grateful to the following for the permissions to reproduce copyright photographs and material:**

Key: l = left, c = centre, r = right, t = top, b = bottom

Alamy/©Image Source Pink for p4(cl), p4(bcl), /©Iain Masterton for p5(tr), /©Blue Jean Images for p6(t), /©PhotoAlto for p6(br), /©David R Frazier Photo Library Inc for p10(tl), / ©Steve Skjold for p10(bl), /©Design Pics Inc for p12(tl), /©Aardvark for p12(cl), /©JTB Communications Inc for p14(l), /©Ellen Isaacs for p14(r), ©Jochen Tack for p16(tl), /©Sarah Hadley for p20(l), /©Keith Morris for p20(r), /©David Angel for p30(tl), /©Blend Images for p35(l), /©Photo Stock-Israel for p37, /©Karen T Spencer for p39(bus), /©Peter Forsberg for p39(pub), /©David Coleman for p39(British Museum), ©Alex Segre for p39(Camden Market), /©GlowImages for p39(b), /©International Photobank for p40(t), /©Tim Ha for p56(b); Corbis/©Simon Jarratt for p4(tr), /©Patrick Lane/Somos Images for p4(bcr), p4(cr), /©Radius for p34, /©Roy Shakespeare/Loop Images for p40(ct), /©Bettmann for p49, /©Christine Schneider/Cultura for p50, /©Geoff Arrow for p55(t), /©Bettmann for p57(tr); Getty/©Photodisc for p4(ccl), p4(cr), /©AFP for p10(tr), /©Photodisc for p10(br), /©DMH Images for p19, /©Photodisc for p29, /©Hulton Archive for p57(b); istockphoto/©Volodymr Kyrylyuk for p5(tl), /©Mitchell Weisberg for p5(tc), /©Daniel Loiselle for p6(bl), /©Nicholas Piccillo for p26(tl), /©Diane Diederich for p27, /©Brian Raisbeck for p36(C), /©Briss for p51, /©bobbieo for p52(ct), /©Janne Ahvo for p52(cb), /©Pathathai Chungyam for p52(b), /©Brad Killer for p56(t); Masterfile/©Peter Griffith for p9(t); PA/©Tony Marshall/ Empics Sport for 57(rcb); Photolibrary/©Superstock for p4(tl), /©Jack Hollingsworth for p4(bl), p4(br), /©Ingram Publishing for p10(bc), /©Westend61 for p12(tr), /©Britain on View for p39(zoo), /©James Winspear for p42(t), /©Jim Craigmyle for p45, /©Burke/Triolo Productions for p52(t); Punchstock/©Juice Images for p54(cb), /©Losevsky Pavel for p56(c); Rex Features for p10(tc), /©Giuliario Bevilacqua for p26(cr); Shutterstock/©Yuri Acurs for p26(cl), /©Helen & Vlad Filatov for p36(D), /©R J Lerich for p36(E), /©Mark William Richardson for p39(Buckingham Palace), /©Alex Young for p39(St Paul's), p40(cb), /©Andrew F Kazmierski for p40(b), /©Mayer George Vladimirovich for p42(c), /©R J Lerich for p42(b), /©Pierdelune for p47, p57(tl); Throckmorton Fine Art, New York for p57(rct); Adrian Doff for p54(b).

**Illustrations by** Kathy Baxendale, Tom Croft, Mark Duffin, Martin Sanders, Nigel Sanderson and Lucy Truman.